HOW TO LIVE
IN A DANGEROUS
WORLD

*A STRATFOR Guide to Protecting Yourself,
Your Family and Your Business*

STRATFOR
GLOBAL INTELLIGENCE

STRATFOR
700 Lavaca Street, Suite 900
Austin, Texas 78701

Printed in the United States of America

The contents of this book originally appeared as STRATFOR *reports*
and advisories, most of which were published
on STRATFOR's *subscription Web site.*

ISBN: 1442153733
EAN-13: 9781442153738

CONTENTS

INTRODUCTION

The terrorist attacks against the United States on Sept. 11, 2001, fundamentally changed the way Americans viewed personal security. Literally out of the blue, fuel- and passenger-laden airliners struck business and governmental landmarks in New York City and Washington, D.C., like guided missiles, killing thousands of Americans. The threat of crime was one thing; most law-abiding Americans believed it could be mitigated by sensible precaution. A spectacular attack by a non-state actor against the World Trade Center and Pentagon was quite another. How does one defend against that?

As the United States assumed a war footing, creating the Department of Homeland Security and invading Afghanistan and Iraq, STRATFOR began covering these developments with keen interest. Our interest was not only at the geopolitical level. The 9/11 attacks were a stark reminder that the world is a dangerous place and that individuals as well as nation-states need to be prepared to defend themselves. Clearly, no government can possibly protect every one of its citizens against every conceivable type of attack. Therefore, people need to assume primary responsibility for their own security. This is even more important when a person is traveling or working in a foreign country where the central government is highly corrupt or incompetent.

To help our readers become more aware of existing and emerging threats and attain some useful level of self-protection, STRATFOR's security team began analyzing risks at home and abroad and issuing advisories on how best to deal with them. This book is a collection of those advisories, going all the way back to Jan. 27, 2004 ("The Militant Threat to Hotels," page 43). In the years since, a lot has changed in the world — and in the so-called "Global War on Terror." The Bush administration's military offensive, although stalled in Iraq, did succeed in isolating al Qaeda's core leadership in the mountains of northwestern Pakistan and limiting its reach. A major effort remains under a new administration to further reduce that threat, stabilize Iraq and Pakistan and roll back the Taliban resurgence in Afghanistan. At the same time, Mexico's increasingly violent campaign against the drug cartels has transformed life along the U.S.-Mexican border and has begun bleeding into the southwestern United States — and beyond.

While the threat of another terrorist attack against the United States may seem more distant now than it was in the aftermath of 9/11, it is clear — almost eight years after the fact — that the world is still a dangerous place and individual self-protection may be more important now than ever. It remains a question of *when* rather than *if* another terrorist attack will occur on U.S. soil, and the terrorist threat overseas is still very real. The threat of crime in the United States, spawned by current economic conditions as well as the drug trade in Mexico, is growing, and the need for security at home and abroad is an issue that will be with us for some time.

With those thoughts in mind, STRATFOR presents the following security reports, most of which originally appeared on our subscription Web site. They are organized under chapter headings and presented in the order in which they were published. There is some overlap from piece to piece and chapter to chapter, since most of the articles were written as individual analyses. Also, some of the information may seem dated, which it is by necessity. These pieces represent some of our best tutorials on personal security since January 2004, less than a year after the U.S. invasion of Iraq. Naturally, some observations are linked to a specific time or event years removed from today's security environment, which continues to evolve. Nevertheless, most of the recommendations and principles are every bit as relevant today as they were when they were written, and none should be considered misleading or counterproductive.

In any case, we hope this collection will provide useful guidance, context and perspective on ways to stay safe in a dangerous world.

STRATFOR
Austin, Texas
April 21, 2009

CHAPTER 1: Planning

The Importance of Knowing the Risks in Advance
Jan. 13, 2006

In today's world, international travel presents certain risks for Westerners, especially in areas of Africa, Asia, Latin America, the former Soviet Union and parts of Eastern Europe where governments have less control, and law and order is not as formally established as in other countries. Certainly, the best chance of remaining out of harm's way while traveling or working abroad is to know and understand — in advance — some of the idiosyncrasies of each country's bureaucracy and the security risks that have been identified. Armed with this knowledge, then, the traveler can take proper precautions.

To that end, the U.S. State Department's Web site (www.travel.state.gov) is an excellent place to begin. The site lists travel warnings issued for countries in which potentially dangerous conditions have been identified. It also provides the current Consular Information Sheets for every foreign country, which contain information on visa requirements, health conditions, crime, unusual currency or entry requirements, any areas of instability and contact information for the U.S. Embassy and consulates. In addition, the site provides a link to a page where travelers can register their personal information with the State Department at no cost, which can make it easier for the government to help during an emergency.

The British and Australian governments have similar Web sites that also are excellent sources of information for their citizens traveling abroad. These sites have similar information as found on the U.S. government's site, but may contain additional information that can be useful to U.S. citizens as well. In addition to government Web sites, private security consulting firms can provide more customized information tailored to a specific location or client.

Common street crime presents the most prevalent risk to travelers abroad — although that by no means is the extent of the threat in many areas. The cardinal rule for travelers is that they should never take anything along they are not prepared to part with. This includes items of extreme value — as well as those of sentimental value. For the business traveler who carries a personal computer, this means leaving back-up discs of all important documents at home.

Large sums of money should not be carried. Cash and credit cards should not all be carried in one wallet or pocket, but dispersed in various pockets. Identification and other important documents should be separate from money. Furthermore, it is important to make copies of passports and other important documents, and leave the originals in a safe location, such as a hotel safe. It also is a good idea to keep a copy of the front page of the passport with the relevant identification information at home with relatives in case of an emergency. Relatives and/or co-workers should be provided a full itinerary before the traveler leaves home, so they can provide at least the basic information to the home office or to the appropriate government agency in case of emergency.

Some countries will react negatively or deny entry if the traveler's passport contains a stamp from certain other countries. Many travelers maintain multiple passports — or request that the visa stamp for a particular country be placed on a separate sheet of paper — in order to keep offending stamps separate. Keep in mind that visa and passport information is primarily used by many host governments to collect intelligence, especially in places such as China, India and Russia. There really is little the law-abiding traveler can do to prevent revealing such information to a foreign government, as traveling with a fake passport is the only alternative and that is never a good idea.

Assessing Threats and Vulnerabilities
May 31, 2006

Personal security services are thriving in the post-Sept. 11 world as more and more top executives seek expert protection. The fact remains, however, that many executives — including those whose work location or professional status would seem to warrant them protection — either prefer not to employ security details or are not afforded them by their employers. With some professional help and a fair amount of work, however, it is possible to create a self-protection system that will greatly enhance one's safety and that of one's family.

Professional security details range from a trained, perhaps armed, driver to full-blown, Secret Service- or Diplomatic Security Service-style arrangements involving numbers of agents, armored cars, a communications system and perhaps other high-tech equipment. A few of the more sophisticated corporate executive protection teams operate "black," blending into the background and relying on keen observation and surprise rather than an overwhelming show of force.

Many executives, however, tend to view some types of protective operations as potentially bad for business, fraught with potential liability exposure and not in keeping with the corporate image they wish to project to the world. Those whose only exposure to protective details is to have witnessed the antics of some details operating in the entertainment business also might find the idea of being surrounded by such protectors personally distasteful.

Having a protective detail can have consequences for one's personal life as well. Privacy and spontaneity are inevitably lost when one is surrounded by people who legitimately need advance knowledge of one's every move. A well-known executive once told a host who asked him to stay on at a party: "I'd love to, but the truth is, if I stay late there are 10 people outside who have to stay late with me." Moreover, the decision to hire protection implies acceptance of the existence of danger, a tough psychological hurdle for many people to overcome — at least, until something bad happens. For all these reasons, many key executives continue to say "no" to protection, regardless of advice and indications to the contrary.

- Baseline surveillance diagnostics. Surveillance diagnostics, a sophisticated blend of several surveillance-detection techniques, are performed by a professional team to determine whether the principal or his/her family is under programmatic hostile surveillance or criminal casing. It concentrates on the home, the school (if applicable), the workplace, any regular venues the principal predictably visits, and the routes between them. This is a "snapshot" to establish a baseline from which to plan, going forward.

- Route analysis. Route analysis looks for vulnerabilities, or choke points, on the principal's regular travel routes. Choke points have two main characteristics: First, they are places where rapid forward motion is difficult, such as sharp blind curves. Second, they are places where hostiles can wait with impunity for their victims. The "best" choke points also offer rapid escape routes for attackers. Choke points are used both by highly professional kidnap/assassination teams, and by criminal "ambush predators" who wait for targets of opportunity. Route analysis is usually done at the same time and by the same team that conducts surveillance diagnostics.

- Physical security surveys. These surveys are performed for the home, work place or school for the principal and family members. Although principals can effectively survey their homes, a professional look is highly recommended. Professionals also should handle any security upgrades that might need to be installed. For surveys and upgrades at workplaces and schools, obviously principals must rely on security resources at those venues.

- Assessment of response capabilities. Also critical is a realistic assessment of the capabilities and responsiveness of local police, other security assets, and fire and medical first responders in the area. It is not sufficient to make assumptions about this; personal security depends critically on knowing whether and under what circumstances help is available, and when it is not.

Armed with a realistic assessment, complete with recommendations, the principal can begin to formulate a personal- and family-protection plan.

Analysis and Planning for Self-Protection
June 1, 2006

No one can be on red alert everywhere and at all times and still expect to live a satisfactory life. Even if one did live in a constant state of hypervigilance, it would be no guarantee of safety. This is true even of executives whose professional status and/or job location might put them in harm's way but who prefer to go without expert security protection or are not provided this service by their companies. By working with know whom to call. In most developed countries, there is some version of the 911 system. In areas where police response and capabilities are not to be trusted, employees and their families may have access to the employer's security control center, which can call out a protective response. If family members are scattered (kids at school, wife at her workplace, husband at his), families should have a preset plan for who calls whom to alert them and ascertain their safety. In some cases, families should have a simple code for communication under duress. This is an easily remembered word or phrase known by all family members that will discreetly signal that one is under duress. For children, "kid phones" traceable via a global positioning system will soon be available.

- Fire and home evacuation. Not all threats are criminal. Principals should have an established plan for evacuating the home and ensuring that all family members are safe.

- Area evacuation. In regions threatened by war, major civil unrest or possible natural disaster, leaving the area during a crisis could be the safest course of action. Principals should have a preset plan in place for accomplishing this successfully.

- Drilling. Emergency plans, even simple ones, cannot be expected to work unless they are practiced periodically. This is not only true in cases involving children. Under sudden stress, people of all ages can experience diminished thought and decision-making processes.

Once the security plan is in place, the principal and his or her family can begin the process of learning the skills to become mentally and physically prepared to successfully handle a threat. This step, training, is the most challenging.

Contingency Plans: An Ounce of Prevention
Aug. 15, 2007

U.S. counterterrorism sources remain concerned that an attack against the U.S. homeland will occur within the next two to three weeks. This is not surprising, considering that the drums have been beating loudly in Washington this summer about a potential attack — first from Homeland Security Secretary Michael Chertoff and then in the form of a National Intelligence Estimate. More recently, several other reports have appeared concerning an impending attack, including an alert over the weekend in New York triggered by an alleged dirty bomb plot.

One reason for the heightened concern is that most everyone, including STRATFOR, is surprised that no major jihadist attack has occurred on U.S. soil since 9/11. Many plots have been disrupted, and it is only a matter of time before one of them succeeds. Simply put, attacks are not difficult to conduct and the government cannot stop them all.

STRATFOR's assessment of the jihadist threat to the U.S. homeland is that al Qaeda and jihadists retain the ability to conduct tactical strikes against the United States but lack the ability to pose a strategic threat. While this may be reassuring on one level, people can and will be killed in a tactical strike. The fact that an attack is not strategically significant will provide no immediate solace to those near the carnage and confusion of a tactical attack. Additionally, as we saw in Hurricane Katrina or the recent bridge collapse in Minneapolis, other disasters also can lead to chaos and disruption.

Given the current threat environment, this is an opportune time to examine again ways to avoid — or at least mitigate — the impact of that chaos and panic. The set of tools designed to do that is called personal contingency planning.

Chaos and Disruption

When disaster strikes, as in a terrorist attack, a number of things happen quickly and simultaneously. Often, panic erupts while people attempt to flee the scene of the attack. At the same time, police, fire and emergency medical units all attempt to respond to the scene, so there can be terrible traffic and pedestrian crowd-control problems. This effect can be magnified by smoke and fire, which can occlude vision, affect breathing and increase panic. Indeed, many of the injuries produced by terrorist bombings are not a direct result of the blast or even shrapnel but of smoke inhalation and trampling.

In many instances, an attack or natural disaster will damage electrical lines, or the electricity will be cut off as a precautionary measure. Elevators also could be reserved for firefighters. This means people are trapped in subway tunnels or in high-rise buildings, and might be forced to escape through smoke-filled tunnels or stairwells. Depending on the incident, bridges, tunnels, subway lines and airports can be closed or merely jammed to a standstill. This gridlock effect might be multiplied if the power is out to traffic signals.

In the midst of this confusion and panic, telephone and cell phone usage soars. Even if the main trunk lines and cell towers are not damaged or otherwise affected by the loss of electricity, this huge spike in activity quickly overloads the exchanges and cell networks. This means the ripples of chaos and disruption roll outward from the scene as people outside the immediate vicinity of the attack zone hear about the attack via the media and wonder what has become of loved ones who were near the site of the attack.

The Importance of Planning

Those in the vicinity of an attack have the best chance of escaping and reconnecting with loved ones if they have a personal contingency plan. Though such planning is critically important for people who live and work in close proximity to known terrorist targets such as Manhattan, Washington and Los Angeles, the recent bridge collapse in Minneapolis has demonstrated that such planning is important for people in other parts of the country as well. Sudden disasters, such as tornados, earthquakes, school a subway tunnel is filling with smoke, you must have the situational awareness to keep low in order to avoid being overcome.

In some cases, evacuation might not be the best idea. If there is no immediate threat to you at your current location, you could run a larger risk of being injured by joining the crowd of panicked people on the street. In some cases, it might be safest to just stay in place and wait for order to return — especially if you are in a location where you have emergency stocks of food and water.

If you work in a high-rise building, frequently travel or take a subway, there are a couple of pieces of equipment that can assist you in case the need to evacuate arises. One of these is a smoke hood, a protective device that fits over the head and provides protection from smoke inhalation. Smoke hoods are relatively inexpensive devices that can be carried in a briefcase or purse and quickly donned in case of emergency. They will usually provide around 20-30 minutes of breathing time — which could quite literally mean the difference between life and death in a smoke-filled hallway, stairway or subway tunnel. The second piece of equipment is a flashlight small enough to fit in a pocket, purse or briefcase. Such a light could prove to be invaluable in a crisis situation at night or when the power goes out in a large building or subway. Some of the small aluminum flashlights also can serve as a handy self-defense weapon.

If you live in an area likely to be hit by such an attack, it also might be prudent to prepare a small "fly-away" kit containing clothes, water, a first-aid kit, nutritional bars, medications and toiletry items for you and your family. It also is a good idea to include a battery-powered radio and other useful items, such as multi-tool knives and duct tape. The kit should be kept in a convenient place, ready to grab on the way out. Even if it is impractical to keep all these items in constant readiness, keeping most of them together and using a prepared list to collect the other items quickly can help get you out the door in seconds. Maintaining important papers, such as vehicle titles, deeds, licenses, birth certificates, passports and credit card information, in a central file allows you to grab that file quickly and take it with you.

The Need for Flexibility

It is important to listen to authorities in the case of an emergency, though you cannot rely on the government to take care of you in every situation because the resources simply are not there to do so. You must have plans ready to take care of yourself and your family.

If you have pets, you will want to take them into consideration when you make your plans. Will Fluffy be taken to the evacuation site in the case of a dirty bomb attack?

The emergency plan also must be fluid and flexible. It is important to recognize that even a good contingency plan can be worthless if protective measures taken by authorities during an emergency impede execution of the plan, or if the catastrophe itself closes down a section of your route. For example, bridges and tunnels might be closed and streets blocked off or jammed with traffic, meaning you might not be able to travel to safety or pick up family members or coworkers. Those whose plan calls for a flight out of the city might be unable to get to the airport or helipad or, once there, find that air traffic has been grounded, as happened after the 9/11 attacks. For these reasons, it is best to have several alternate contingency plans that account for multiple scenarios and include various evacuation routes. Once the emergency is announced, it likely is too late to start devising a plan.

Plans must be reviewed periodically. A plan made following 9/11 might no longer be valid. Bridges and roads you included might now be closed for construction. If Uncle Al's place in West Virginia is your planned communications hub, then that needs to change when he moves to Texas.

Your equipment also should be checked periodically to ensure it is functional. Have you checked the batteries in your flashlight? Has your smoke hood become battered from being carried around for too many years? Have the power bars in your fly-away kit become fossilized?

Finally, while having a contingency plan on paper is better than having nothing, those that are tested in the real world are far superior. Running through an evacuation plan (especially during a high-traffic time such as rush hour) will help identify weaknesses that will not appear on paper. It also will help to ensure that all those involved know what they are supposed to do and where they are supposed to go. A plan is of limited use if half of the people it is designed for do not understand their respective roles and responsibilities.

No plan is perfect, and chances are you will have to "shift on the fly" and change your plan in the event of an actual emergency. However, having a plan — and being prepared — will allow you to be more focused and less panicked and confused than those who have left their fate to chance. In life and death situations, an ounce of prevention is a good thing.

CHAPTER 2: Situational Awareness

Guarding Cash and ATM Transactions
Jan. 23, 2006

Robbers, pickpockets, kidnappers and other criminals — not only in developing countries — tend to target traveling Westerners because of a general belief that their pockets are filled with cash or that they have access to large sums of money. Indeed, when traveling abroad, tourists and businesspeople often find it necessary to carry large amounts of cash or to frequently use ATM cards. To minimize the risk of being robbed — or worse — travelers can take several precautions.

Perhaps the best way to avoid being robbed while in a foreign country is to maintain a low profile. Travelers who wear flashy jewelry or pull out a large wad of cash in public are walking advertisements for victimization. It is best to leave jewelry in the hotel room or, better yet, at home. If it is necessary to carry large amounts of cash, the best practice is to keep it in several locations, and not all in one wallet or purse. A moderate amount of cash, say around $50, kept in a front pocket can be handed over to an assailant should the traveler be confronted. The thinking is that a robber will take the money and run, and the whole confrontation will be over in seconds. The key in this case is to minimize contact with the assailant.

When using an ATM, travelers tend to focus on the task at hand, not so much on those who could be lying in wait. This lack of situational awareness can lead to robbery or, even worse, to an "express" kidnapping [see Chapter 4, page 95], in which the victim is abducted and forced to withdraw money from his or her bank account using his ATM card until the balance is exhausted. Kidnappers who discover there is a large balance in the account have been known to hold on to the traveler until the account is depleted — often stuffed in the trunk of their car. To minimize this danger, many travelers choose to travel with a prepaid bank card — usually obtained at one's local bank — that has a limited amount of money in the account. Having the bank card's international assistance number in a secure location is helpful in the event an ATM card is stolen.

The best location for ATM use is a secure location such as inside a bank or hotel lobby. Many hotels abroad also will process cash advances from the traveler's credit card account or exchange U.S. dollars into local currencies. Traveler's checks also can reduce dependence on ATM's altogether. The key to avoid using ATMs at risky times or in risky locations is to plan ahead, and have correct amount of cash needed for the day's or night's activities.

An increasingly prevalent type of high-tech fraud at ATMs is "skimming." This crime involves placing a device that looks like part of the machine over the card slot. The device contains a card reader that records account information when the ATM machine is used, allowing cybercriminals access to bank account information. In many cases a camera also is placed on the machine to record PIN numbers.

The exchange rate in some countries — which can be artificially skewed in the host country's favor — could tempt some travelers to take part in informal currency exchanges on the street or even in established places of business that are unauthorized to change cash. Visitors who engage in such illegal practices put themselves at risk of being deported — or worse — being jailed in some cases. This practice also opens up the possibility of receiving counterfeit money, which further puts the traveler at risk of ending up on the wrong side of the law. Being caught exchanging money on the black market can give some governments a means to blackmail foreign executives, forcing them to commit industrial espionage on their companies or face the consequences.

Exchanging money on the street also can put the traveler in close proximity to the local criminal element, which is often tied to organized crime. What starts out as an informal money exchange can easily end up becoming a kidnapping scenario. Generally speaking, if the exchange rate offered by someone on the street sounds too good to be true, it is.

Maintaining situational awareness at all times — at home or abroad — is key to minimizing risks of all kind. While in a strange city, however, travelers can reduce the chances of becoming a victim while away from home by being aware of their surroundings and taking certain precautions.

Key Steps to Avoid Falling Victim to Crime
June 5, 2006

A 35-year-old man awaited trial in Alabama on June 5 following his indictment on five felony counts in connection with the armed abduction and sexual assault of Birmingham lawyer Sandra Eubank Gregory. The suspect, Dedrick Griham, allegedly took Gregory from the parking lot of her apartment complex the morning of May 31 and forced her to make cash withdrawals from a series of ATMs. Details on the case, including surveillance video of the abduction, clearly indicate this began as an "express kidnapping."

Common in Third World countries but unusual in the United States, express kidnappings are easy to perpetrate and often last only a few hours. In Gregory's case, Griham allegedly took her by surprise in broad daylight, pulling a gun on her from behind as she fumbled in her purse while exiting her car. After forcing her back into the car, her boyfriend's Lexus RX300, the gunman forced Gregory to withdraw cash from three different ATMs. Police arrested Griham and rescued Gregory at a Comfort Inn motel nine hours after the abduction. The two apparently had never met prior to the incident, and it appears that Gregory was simply chosen at random.

Video of the crime scene suggests the 34-year-old Gregory made two mistakes during the initial moments of the kidnapping: She apparently failed to practice situational awareness and she let herself be taken from the primary crime scene.

Being aware of one's surroundings is paramount in this day and age — so much so that it should be routine in everyday life. This is especially true because criminals tend to select victims who are not paying attention, and tend to shy away from those who have made eye contact. This kidnapping only highlights the fact that even in a downtown apartment complex in broad daylight, an unaware person can easily be taken by surprise. Although a large pickup truck in the next parking space may have obscured the kidnapper's approach until he and the victim were virtually face-to-face, it probably did not help that Gregory was looking into her purse instead of checking her surroundings.

People who are not familiar with an area, tourists for instance, can be easy targets for criminals because they may be more focused on the surrounding scenery and not on the people. But people also can become targets in their usual surroundings precisely because they are in familiar territory and thus assume they are safe. In the Gregory case, the attacker did not simply "appear from nowhere," as victims often are tempted to say. Since he approached the victim on foot, he doubtless was waiting nearby, casing for someone to grab. Gregory probably saw her attacker before he approached her. The question is whether she noticed him, and what she might have done differently if she had.

Perhaps Gregory's biggest mistake was allowing herself to be taken from the parking lot. A victim has the greatest chance of survival during the first moments of a kidnapping, making his or her reaction during this brief period crucial. Once victims are taken to a secondary crime scene, they no longer are in a familiar setting and are less likely to be able to obtain help — and so the advantage falls to the kidnapper. Statistics clearly show that resistance and escape, even when facing a firearm, yields better odds of survival than going to a secondary crime scene. In this case, just as the suspect was backing Gregory's car out of her parking spot, a second woman entered the lot. If Gregory had only delayed a few moments longer or screamed for help, the second woman might have been able to, at the very least, summon help. As a general rule, then, victims should resist an assailant's attempts to force them into a vehicle, even one belonging to the victim. In this case, the assailant was only a robber. Had he been a sexual predator or a killer, he would have had ample time to commit his more violent crime.

The best way to avoid becoming a victim is to be aware of potential threats in the immediate vicinity and take proactive measures against them. By establishing early eye contact with potential assailants, people often can ward off attacks, as this small gesture communicates a nonsubmissive posture without being overtly confrontational. Most criminals seeking a target of opportunity will target a victim that displays less-assertive behavior. In interviews with law enforcement after a crime, many victims report they had felt something was wrong, or had a bad feeling about their assailant immediately before the attack, but that they took no preventive measures such as crossing the street or taking some other evasive action. Trusting one's instincts or "inner voice" and not allowing one's denial to override common sense often is the best way to avoid becoming a victim.

Threats, Situational Awareness and Perspective
Aug. 22, 2007

In last week's Terrorism Intelligence Report, we said U.S. counterterrorism sources remain concerned an attack will occur on U.S. soil in the next few weeks. Although we are skeptical of these reports, al Qaeda and other jihadists do retain the ability — and the burning desire — to conduct tactical strikes within the United States. One thing we did not say last week, however, was that we publish such reports not to frighten readers but to impress upon them the need for preparedness, which does not mean paranoia.

Fear and paranoia, in fact, are counterproductive to good personal and national security. As such, we have attempted over the past few years to place what we consider hyped threats into the proper perspective. To this end, we have addressed threats such as al Qaeda's chemical and biological weapons capabilities, reports of a looming "American Hiroshima" nuclear attack against the United States, the dirty bomb threat, the smoky bomb threat, and the threat of so-called "mubtakkar devices," among others.

Though some threats are indeed hyped, the world nonetheless remains a dangerous place. Undoubtedly, at this very moment some people are seeking ways to carry out attacks against targets in the United States. Moreover, terrorism attacks are not the only threat — far more people are victimized by common criminals. Does this reality mean that people need to live in constant fear and paranoia? Not at all. If people do live that way, those who seek to terrorize them have won. However, by taking a few relatively simple precautions and adjusting their mindsets, people can live

32

less-stressful lives during these uncertain times. One of the keys to personal preparedness and protection is to have a contingency plan in place in the event of an attack or other major emergency. The second element is practicing situational awareness.

The Proper State of Mind

Situational awareness is the process of recognizing a threat at an early stage and taking measures to avoid it. Being observant of one's surroundings and identifying potential threats and dangerous situations is more of an attitude or mindset than it is a hard skill. Because of this, situational awareness is not just a process that can be practiced by highly trained government agents or specialized corporate security countersurveillance teams — it can be adopted and employed by anyone.

An important element of this mindset is first coming to the realization that a threat exists. Ignorance or denial of a threat — or completely tuning out to one's surroundings while in a public place — makes a person's chances of quickly recognizing the threat and avoiding it slim to none. This is why apathy, denial and complacency are so deadly.

An example is the case of Terry Anderson, the Associated Press bureau chief in Lebanon who was kidnapped on March 16, 1985. The day before his abduction, Anderson was driving in Beirut traffic when a car pulled in front of his and nearly blocked him in. Due to the traffic situation, and undoubtedly a bit of luck, Anderson was able to avoid what he thought was an automobile accident — even though events like these can be hallmarks of preoperational planning. The next day, Anderson's luck ran out as the same vehicle successfully blocked his vehicle in the same spot. Anderson was pulled from his vehicle at gunpoint — and held hostage for six years and nine months.

Clearly, few of us are living in the type of civil war conditions that Anderson faced in 1985 Beirut. Nonetheless, average citizens face all kinds of threats today — from common thieves and assailants to criminals and mentally disturbed individuals who aim to conduct violent acts in the school, mall or workplace, to militants wanting to carry out large-scale attacks. Should an attack occur, a person with a complacent or apathetic mindset will be taken completely by surprise and could freeze up in shock and denial as his or her mind is forced to quickly adjust to a newly recognized and unforeseen situational. That person is in no condition to react, flee or resist.

Denial and complacency, however, are not the only hazardous states of mind. As mentioned above, paranoia and obsessive concern about one's safety and security can be just as dangerous. There are times when it is important to be on heightened alert — a woman walking alone in a dark parking lot is one example — but people are simply not designed to operate in a state of heightened awareness for extended periods of time. The body's "flight or fight" response is helpful in a sudden emergency, but a constant stream of adrenalin and stress leads to mental and physical burnout. It is very hard for people to be aware of their surroundings when they are completely fried.

Situational awareness, then, is best practiced at a balanced level referred to as "relaxed awareness," a state of mind that can be maintained indefinitely without all the stress associated with being on constant alert. Relaxed awareness is not tiring, and allows people to enjoy life while paying attention to their surroundings.

When people are in a state of relaxed awareness, it is far easier to make the transition to a state of heightened awareness than it is to jump all the way from complacency to heightened awareness. So, if something out of the ordinary occurs, those practicing relaxed awareness can heighten their awareness while they attempt to determine whether the anomaly is indeed a threat. If it is, they can take action to avoid it; if it is not, they can stand down and return to a state of relaxed awareness.

Telltale Signs

What are we looking for while we are in a state of relaxed awareness? Essentially the same things we discussed when we described what bad surveillance looks like. It is important to remember that almost every criminal act, from a purse-snatching to a terrorist bombing, involves some degree of preoperational surveillance and that criminals are vulnerable to detection during that time. This is because criminals, even militants planning terrorist attacks, often are quite sloppy when they are casing their intended targets. They have been able to get away with their sloppy practices for so long because most people simply do not look for them. On the positive side, however, that also means that people who are looking can spot them fairly easily.

The U.S. government uses the acronym TEDD to illustrate the principles one can use to identify surveillance, but these same principles also can be used to identify criminal threats. TEDD stands for time, environment, distance and demeanor. In other words, if a person sees someone repeatedly over time, in different environments and over distance, or one who displays poor demeanor, then that person can assume he or she is under surveillance. If a person is the specific target of a planned attack, he or she might be exposed to the time, environment and distance elements of TEDD, but if the subway car the person is riding in or the building where the person works is the target, he or she might only have the element of demeanor to key on. This also is true in the case of criminals who behave like "ambush predators" and lurk in an area waiting for a victim. Because their attack cycle is extremely condensed, the most important element to watch for is demeanor.

By poor demeanor, we simply mean a person is acting unnaturally. This behavior can look blatantly suspicious, such as someone who is lurking and/or has no reason for being where he is or for doing what he is doing. Sometimes, however, poor demeanor can be more subtle, encompassing almost imperceptible behaviors that the target senses more than observes. Other giveaways include moving when the target moves, communicating when the target moves, avoiding eye contact with the target, making sudden turns or stops, or even using hand signals to communicate with other members of a surveillance team.

In the terrorism realm, exhibiting poor demeanor also can include wearing unseasonably warm clothing, such as trench coats in the summer; displaying odd bulges under clothing or wires protruding from clothing; unnaturally sweating, mumbling or fidgeting; or attempting to avoid security personnel. In addition, according to some reports, suicide bombers often exhibit an intense stare as they approach the final stages of their mission. They seem to have tunnel vision, being able to focus only on their intended target.

Perspective

We have seen no hard intelligence that supports the assertions that a jihadist attack will occur in the next few weeks and are somewhat skeptical about such reports. Regardless of whether our U.S. counterterrorism sources are correct this time, though, the world remains a dangerous place. Al Qaeda, grassroots jihadists and domestic militants of several different political persuasions have the desire and capability to conduct attacks. Meanwhile, criminals and mentally disturbed individuals, such as the Virginia Tech shooter, appear to be getting more violent every day.

In the big picture, violence and terrorism have always been a part of the human condition. The Chinese built the Great Wall for a reason other than tourism. Today's "terrorists" are far less dangerous to society as a whole than were the Viking berserkers and barbarian tribes who terrorized Europe for centuries, and the ragtag collection of men who have sworn allegiance to Osama bin Laden pose far less of a threat to Western civilization than the large, battle-hardened army Abdul Rahman al-Ghafiqi led into the heart of France in 732.

Terrorist attacks are designed to have a psychological impact that far outweighs the actual physical damage caused by the attack itself. Denying the perpetrators this multiplication effect — as the British did after the July 2005 subway bombings — prevents them from accomplishing their greater goals. Therefore, people should prepare, plan and practice relaxed awareness — and not let paranoia and the fear of terrorism and crime rob them of the joy of life.

Terrorist Targets and the Lifesaving Mindset
Oct. 27, 2005

In our recent series on the terrorist attack cycle, we noted that terrorist and criminal operatives planning an attack are most vulnerable while conducting preoperational surveillance. Once the operation progresses to the attack phase, it generally is too late to stop it. Terrorists will have seen the target's security measures during their surveillance and will have factored them into their operational planning. If they are unable to develop a tactic to counter the target's protective security measures — or deploy enough firepower to overwhelm the measures — they simply will choose an easier target.

By the attack phase, the attackers have identified the time and place in which their intended target is most vulnerable and have gathered the personnel and weapons required for the strike. In other words, they now have the luxury of choosing the precise time, place and method of attack — giving them the element of tactical surprise. They also will have prepared overwhelming firepower, such as a large improvised explosive device (IED), if the operation calls for it.

Given the attackers' advantages, only a few factors can prevent a successful attack. The first is simple human error, often due to inexperience. On Dec. 22, 2001, Richard Reid was able to achieve tactical surprise by sneaking a shoe filled with explosives onto American Airlines flight 63. Between Paris and Miami Reid attempted to light his shoe with a match, but an alert flight attendant intervened in time. Reid's inexperience in quickly and properly lighting a piece of safety fuse — and his failure to carry out his task in a locked restroom — saved the flight.

Equipment malfunction also can work against the terrorists. On Jan. 19, 2001, two Iraqi intelligence officers prepared to place an IED at the Thomas Jefferson Cultural Center in Manila, Philippines. Teams of intelligence officers had been dispatched from Baghdad to several parts of the world using consecutively numbered Iraqi passports. Their explosives were shipped via the diplomatic pouch and their operations coordinated by Iraqi embassies in their respective countries. By attacking the U.S. government in the Philippines instead of in some expected place such as Istanbul, Turkey, or Riyadh, Saudi Arabia, the Iraqis achieved tactical surprise. Unfortunately for the officers, as they pushed the button to activate the timer, the device cooked off instantaneously, killing one of them and severely wounding the other. An identical device placed at the U.S. ambassador's residence in Jakarta, Indonesia, failed to detonate.

The third factor is the target's plain luck. On March 15, 1985, the vehicle driven by Terry Anderson, who at the time was The Associated Press bureau chief in Beirut, Lebanon, was nearly blocked by a car that pulled in front of it. Due to a number of traffic factors, Anderson was able to avoid what he thought was an automobile accident and continue on his way. The next day, Anderson's luck ran out as the same vehicle successfully blocked his vehicle in the same spot. Anderson was pulled from his vehicle at gunpoint — and held hostage for six years and nine months.

Although intended targets have almost no control over the abovementioned factors, they do not have to resign themselves to being "sitting ducks" — if they employ attack recognition.

The most vital aspect of attack recognition is the target's mental mindset. If a target remains unaware of the surroundings and oblivious to the fact that he is a potential target, his chances of recognizing the attack and taking countermeasures — and thus surviving — are very slim. A target in the it-will-never-happen-to-me frame of mind usually will go into shock — and freeze — as the attack begins.

This is not to encourage paranoia. One cannot function for long in that mental state, as extreme situational awareness and fear lead to a quick burnout. However, potential targets, such as U.S. businesspeople in a critical terrorism or crime environment, must maintain a heightened state of situational awareness. Only by paying attention to the people and events in the vicinity — whether one is walking, driving or riding a subway or in a chauffeur-driven car — can one begin to take evasive measures in time to possibly prevent an attack.

Victims of abductions and attempted assassinations many times are able to describe in detail — and in retrospect — how they were surveilled. They also acknowledge having had indications that they were about to be attacked, such as bad feelings about particular people or situations. Because of their mindset at the time, however, they failed to heed the warning signs and take action.

Not all of these indications will be as blatant as the failed abduction attempt against Anderson, but certain signs can indicate that something is afoot. One such sign is an operational signal. Quite often the attack team will employ a spotter to positively identify the target and alert the team that the target is entering the attack site. This signaling can be done by hand, with vehicle headlights or radios. Cell phones can be used but are not fast enough in many situations. Another sign could be a broken down vehicle or some other event or person who seems out of place.

Also, it is important in successful attack recognition to analyze the potential target to determine where vulnerabilities exist. This analysis should look at schedules and routes to determine predictable patterns. It also should identify potential choke points — places along a normal travel route that give the hostile elements the ability to control the target, provide cover for their actions and escape. Particular attention should then be paid to people, objects and events in and around the choke points and other possible attack sites. This often is where hostile surveillance or elements of an impending attack can be detected before the hostiles can spring their trap.

Of course, recognizing that something is amiss is just the first step. The second step is action. This can be as simple as following one's instincts. If something "feels" wrong to the target, even if he or she cannot articulate the problem, some action should be taken — even if it means simply turning off the road and avoiding a choke point.

More important, if the potential target senses an attack coming, or actually is attacked, they must not let themselves slip into shock, freeze and panic. We call this "getting off the X." The attackers already have selected the ideal attack site — the X — and the target cannot just sit on it. The target must fight back.

Many government and private training courses are available that teach tactical driving techniques and personal defense skills for "getting off the X." No amount of training, however, can save even highly trained targets if they freeze up in an attack situation. It also is important to realize that solutions to every problem cannot be taught. Classrooms and practical exercises can only simulate a limited number of scenarios. When confronted in the real world by a life-or-death scenario, improvisation often is necessary.

The same principles also apply to IED attacks. Certainly the flight attendant on Reid's flight realized what was going on and quickly rallied the passengers to restrain him and prevent him from lighting his device. Recognizing that a possible IED attack is in progress and avoiding the attack zone by driving, running, ducking or diving for cover is vital.

CHAPTER 3: Various Venues

The Militant Threat to Hotels
Jan. 27, 2004

Islamist militants are changing the way they do business. With the "hardening" of security around high-value targets worldwide that followed the Sept. 11 attacks, militants increasingly have turned their attention to "soft targets," which include hotels. From the jihadist viewpoint, Western hotel chains and large luxury hotels could become the next best targets to embassies — they are symbols of Western elitism and offer excellent opportunities to strike at Westerners on foreign soil. And unlike government-protected embassies, most hotels remain easily accessible for preoperational surveillance and attacks, as demonstrated by bombings in Mombassa, Jakarta, Casablanca and, most recently, Egypt's Sinai Peninsula.

Though the most likely method of attack at a hotel would involve a car or truck bomb or a suicide bomb in a public area, the risk to Westerners of being kidnapped or assassinated by Islamist militants is growing — and hotels are a venue for these crimes as well. Past plots demonstrate that such plans may be highly sophisticated.

These threats present serious considerations for corporate executives in the hotel and hospitality industry. Beyond the obvious necessity of protecting guests and employees, taking pre-emptive security measures is emerging as a corporate legal imperative, with failure to do so opening companies up to the possibility of damaging litigation.

Hotel operators have numerous methods to limit threats and deflect the interest of militant groups. In addition to important physical security measures like vehicle barricades and window film, employee training and protective countersurveillance programs are invaluable tools for securing a property.

Resources need to be spread evenly over all properties. In fact, geography is a key factor in determining the threat level to a particular hotel. The highest threats to hotels exist in Muslim countries with a known militant presence; such threats are somewhat lower in Western countries, including the United States. Vulnerability assessments of properties are a key method for determining how to best deploy finite resources to reduce the risk of a terrorist event.

The Emergence of Soft Targets

One of the important outgrowths of the Sept. 11 attacks was the substantial increase in security measures and countersurveillance around U.S. government and military facilities in the United States and overseas. The attacks had a similar impact in U.S. and foreign airports. The effective "hardening" of such facilities — which top the list of preferred militant targets — has made it measurably more difficult for militants to carry out large-scale strikes in these areas.

As a result, potential target sets have shifted from government and military facilities to lower-profile "soft targets" — defined generally as public or semi-public facilities where large numbers of people congregate under relatively loose security. Soft targets include various forms of public transportation, shopping malls, corporate offices, places of worship, schools and sports venues, to name a few.

Generally speaking, soft targets are easily accessible areas: They attract high human traffic and are surrounded by small security perimeters — often limited to gates and poorly trained guards — if perimeters exist at all. They are noteworthy for their dearth of trained, professional security personnel, actionable intelligence on potential threats and countersurveillance measures. The combination makes for an attractive target in the eyes of a militant.

Between the first World Trade Center bombing on Feb. 26, 1993, and the second attack on Sept. 11, 2001, al Qaeda focused primarily on hitting hard targets, including:

- A U.S.-Saudi military facility in Riyadh, Saudi Arabia. Seven people, including five Americans, were killed when two bombs exploded on Nov. 13, 1995.

- A U.S. military base near Dhahran, Saudi Arabia. A bomb killed 19 U.S. soldiers and wounded hundreds of Americans and Saudis on June 25, 1996.

- U.S. embassies in Nairobi, Kenya, and Dar es Salaam, Tanzania. More than 250 people were killed and 5,000 injured in the Aug. 7, 1998, bombings.

- The USS Cole. Seventeen sailors were killed in the Oct. 12, 2000, attack in Yemen.

Following Sept. 11, there was a marked shift in attacks that was consistent with one of al Qaeda's key strengths — adaptability. Al Qaeda-linked militant strikes since that time read like a laundry list of soft targets:

- April 11, 2002. The firebombing of a synagogue in Tunisia kills 19. The Abu Hafs al-Masri Brigades, an al Qaeda subgroup, claims responsibility.

- Oct. 12, 2002. Jemaah Islamiyah stages a pair of bombings at a nightclub in Bali, Indonesia, killing 202 people.

- Nov. 28, 2002. The bombing of the Israeli-owned Paradise Hotel in Mombassa, Kenya, kills 13. An attempt to shoot down an Israeli charter jet with a surface-to-air missile at Mombassa airport is unsuccessful. Both incidents are believed to be the work of al Qaeda's operational center in east Africa.

- May 12, 2003. Suicide bombers attack a housing complex in Riyadh, Saudi Arabia, killing 34 people, including 10 Americans.

- May 16, 2003. A series of bomb attacks in Casablanca, Morocco, targeting a Jewish community center, a Spanish restaurant and social club, a hotel and the Belgian consulate, kill 41.

- Aug. 5, 2003. A suicide bomber affiliated with Jemaah Islamiyah kills 12 people at the JW Marriott Hotel in Jakarta, Indonesia.

- Nov. 8, 2003. Suicide bombers strike a Saudi residential complex in Riyadh, killing 17 people.

- Nov. 15, 2003. Twenty-six people are killed in bombings of synagogues in Istanbul, Turkey. The Abu Hafs al-Masri Brigades claim responsibility.

- March 11, 2004. Multiple explosions hit the rail system in Madrid, killing nearly 200 people and injuring about 1,800. The Abu Hafs al-Masri Brigades claims responsibility.

- May 1, 2004. A team of four militants attack a Western corporate office in Yanbu, Saudi Arabia, killing six people.

- May 29, 2004. A team of four militants attack several Western corporate offices and housing compounds in al-Khobar, Saudi Arabia, taking hostages and killing 22 people.

- Oct. 7, 2004. At least 22 people are killed when an vehicle into the lobby of the Hilton Hotel in Taba, Egypt, a resort town on the Sinai Peninsula, and another suicide bomber detonates explosives in the pool area moments later. Separately, two car bombs also are detonated at campsites near Nuweba. Israelis are targeted in all incidents.

While there have also been attacks since Sept. 11 against harder targets such as embassies, the trend toward softer targets is unmistakable. This trend will continue as Islamist militant cells become even more autonomous, and with the growth of "freelance" jihadists in various parts of the world. These are al Qaeda sympathizers inspired by Sept. 11, Afghanistan, Iraq or some other event but who lack specific training in camps and likely have no direct connection to the wider jihadist network. Nevertheless, they can be dangerous, particularly if they are attempting to prove their value. In both cases, a lack of resources, planning capabilities and operational experience will necessitate the choice of softer targets.

Hitting such targets allows militants to maximize the casualty count while limiting the chance of preoperational interdiction. This is a question of access to the target as well as limited or ineffective countersurveillance.

From a militant perspective, the downside is that hitting soft targets usually limits the political and ideological mileage of the attack. Islamist militants prefer targets with high symbolic value, but they have proved willing to forego some degree of symbolism in exchange for a higher chance of success. However, attacks against certain soft targets, such as synagogues and large Western hotels, can at times provide the necessary combination of symbolism and a large — primarily Western — body count.

The Threat to Hotels

Hotels — particularly large, Western-owned hotels on foreign soil — are the quintessential "soft target." They have fixed locations and daily business activity that creates a perfect cover for pre-operative surveillance. Extensive traffic — both human and vehicular, inside and outside the buildings — goes largely unregulated. This is especially true for larger hotels that incorporate bars, restaurants, clubs, shops and other public facilities. While security workers do monitor and confront suspicious loiterers, one easy work-around for militants is simply to check into the hotel, thereby gaining full access and guest privileges.

The ingress and egress gives militants ample opportunity to blend into the crowd, both for extensive preoperational surveillance and actual strikes. In a departure from the security situation in airports and other places, it is not uncommon to see anonymous and unattended baggage.

Outside, most hotel perimeters are unsecured, with limited to non-existent standoff distance and easy access for cars and trucks — including buses and taxis that could be used as a Trojan horse for a bombing. Also, it is common for vehicles to be parked and left unattended in front of many hotels. Loading ramps and parking garages offer other opportunities for those seeking to detonate large truck or car bombs.

Ultimately, security rests primarily in the hands of hotel workers. Globally, police and other government security forces are stretched thin; their priority is to protect official VIPs and critical infrastructure. Threats to hotels and other private facilities are of secondary concern, at best.

However, many large hotels and hotel chains are unwilling to incur the direct costs associated with hardening security, such as more numerous and better-trained guards. Though some hotels have expanded the use of video surveillance, most lack the trained professionals and man hours needed to turn electronic gadgets into intelligence tools. In most cases, the utility of the technology comes after an attack, during the investigative phase, and thus has little preventive value. Similarly, guards and other employees are rarely trained in countersurveillance techniques, which may be the most cost-effective method of preventing an attack.

In the past, many hotel managers have been unwilling to risk alienating their clientele by incorporating more cumbersome security measures — such as identity and key checks upon entry, baggage screening and more extensive standoff areas — that guests view as inconvenient and which thus could directly impact business. Moreover, it can be difficult to justify the investment of millions of dollars in security precautions when the risk — much less the return — cannot be quantified. Given the highly competitive nature of the industry and guests' unwillingness to accept inconvenient security practices, hotel owners often have been forced to take the calculated risk that their businesses will not be targeted.

In the wake of the October 2004 attacks at the Hilton hotel on the Sinai Peninsula, however, that might be changing: An attorney representing some victims has demanded that the Hilton hotel chain accept responsibility for the security and belongings of its guests. Terrorism-related liability considerations, which perhaps could be termed a hushed concern among hotel industry insiders since Sept. 11, are becoming a much more prominent issue. On the upside, there are unique methods of countersurveillance that can help mitigate threats to hotels.

From the jihadist viewpoint, there are several more advantages to targeting hotels. In many countries where militants are numerous, large hotels are among the most prominent symbols of Western culture — especially recognized Western chains such as Marriott, Hilton and Inter-Continental hotels. Also, Islamists long have looked upon hotels as places of vice: They are places where men and women mix freely, and guests can engage in the consumption of alcohol, music and dance, fornication and adultery. This provides an additional, ideological justification for attacking hotels.

Because large hotels are places where Westerners are most likely to be found — either in residence or living or attending meetings, parties or conferences — they offer the best opportunity for militants in many countries to kill or injure large numbers of Westerners, possibly including visiting business and government leaders, in a single attack. Such elites are particularly high-value targets, especially if they are seen as collaborating with or supporting "illegitimate" or "apostate" rulers in Islamic countries such as Pakistan, Saudi Arabia or Jordan.

In Issue No. 7 of al Qaeda's online training manual, Camp al-Bataar Magazine (issued in March 2004), an article providing guidance for striking human targets noted: "The primary targets should be Jews and Christians who have important status in the Islamic countries . . . Our advice is to start with unprotected soft targets and the individuals from countries that support the local renegades." Hotels may well be the best way of attacking Jews and Christians who are visiting and collaborating with local regimes.

Additionally, jihadists increasingly have shown an interest in attacks that carry economic impacts. Spectacular attacks against hotels in certain countries — especially those with tourism-based economies — can generate substantial economic pain. One example is the 2002 nightclub bombings in Bali, Indonesia, which temporarily decimated the island's tourism trade and impacted the wider Southeast Asian tourism industry. The bombing of the Paradise Hotel in Mombassa, Kenya, in 2002 and of the JW Marriott Hotel in Jakarta, Indonesia, the following year had similar impacts, resulting in government travel warnings that cut into those countries' economies. Elsewhere, Egypt's Muslim Brotherhood and ETA in Spain also have struck at hotels and tourist sites as a means of harming the economy and pressuring the enemy governments, a factor that also was at issue in the recent bombings in Sinai.

Bombings: The Primary Threat

Hotels figure prominently in a growing list of successful attacks, with two main types of operations: car and truck bombings and human suicide bombings. Assassinations and kidnappings at hotels also should be considered as a growing risk for Westerners. The most substantial threat comes from bombs: either a car or truck bombing at a hotel entrance, inside a garage or other perimeter locations, or a suicide bomber who seeks to detonate his explosives within a hotel lobby, restaurant or other public gathering place inside a hotel.

Vehicle bombings tend to generate the greatest number of casualties — and they are difficult to defend against, especially without some type of countersurveillance program. Recent car or truck bombings involving hotels as targets have occurred in Jakarta, Indonesia (August 2003); Costa del Sol, Spain (July 2003); Mombassa, Kenya (November 2002); Karachi, Pakistan (May 2002); and Taba, Egypt (October 2004), as well as on multiple occasions during the past year in Iraq.

Suicide bombings or human-placed bombs have occurred inside and outside hotels recently in Katmandu, Nepal (August 2004); Moscow, Russia (December 2003); Casablanca, Morocco (May 2003); Bogota, Colombia (December 2002); Netanya, Israel (March 2002); Jerusalem, Israel (December 2001); and Phnom Penh, Cambodia (July 2001).

In both types of attacks, the majority of those killed or injured were just inside and outside of the hotel lobbies and on the ground floors, with some impact also to the hotels' lower floors. Many of the deaths and injuries result from flying glass, making window film a cheap and effective way of lowering the death toll.

Kidnappings and Assassinations

While bombings remain al Qaeda's favored tactic globally, kidnappings and assassinations are increasing in number as other Islamist militants adapt their tactics. As recent events in Saudi Arabia, Iraq, Pakistan, Chechnya and the Philippines have shown, jihadists have begun to adopt kidnappings — often followed by murder — both as a symbolic act and as a practical means of raising funds.

The editions of Camp al-Bataar Magazine issued in April and May 2004 give very detailed tactical recommendations for carrying out assassinations and kidnappings. Related targeting guidance has placed increased emphasis on symbolic individuals, including Western executives. This certainly does not preclude lower-level employees of Western companies from becoming targets as well.

Hotels, with their substantial traffic and relatively uncontrolled environments, are a prime venue for kidnappings or assassinations. Even high-profile, protected individuals who have constant security protection while traveling generally are more vulnerable at the hotel than elsewhere.

Though security teams can be deployed ahead of time to protect the sites that VIPs visit during the day, individuals tend to be at greatest risk while entering or leaving hotels — which, again, are high-traffic, high-risk environments. Moreover, in such a location, it would be possible for a guest to be kidnapped or killed without anyone noticing his or her absence for some period of time. Sophisticated attacks could be carried out at hotels, where a VIPs location remains static for the longest period of time.

The creativity or planning that al Qaeda could employ in an attack against a VIP at a hotel should not be underestimated. And the threat of a hotel-based assassination of a VIP is not just theoretical: In fact, hotels have been on al Qaeda's radar screen for more than a decade.

The New York City Bomb Plots

In the aftermath of the first World Trade Center bombing in 1993, several plots were uncovered that centered around attacks against the U.N. Plaza Hotel and the Waldorf Astoria Hotel in New York City. Extensive surveillance of the hotel had been conducted — both inside and out — and various attack scenarios were outlined by Ramzi Yousef (the mastermind of the WTC bombing) and the local militant cell. As past experience testifies, it would be foolish to discount these plans today; al Qaeda is known to return to past targets and plot scenarios.

In the New York cases, operatives had devised the following scenarios:

- Using a stolen delivery van, an attack team would drive the wrong way down a one-way street near the Waldorf "well," where VIP motorcades arrived. A hand grenade would be tossed as a diversionary tactic by a lone operative from the church across the street. A four- man assault team (a tactic recently used in Saudi Arabia) would deploy from the rear of the van and attack the protection cars and then the VIP's limousine.

- Another scenario involved militants in gas masks infiltrating the hotel after midnight — when they knew protection levels were lower — moving up to the VIP's floor via the stairwells with assault weapons, hand grenades and tear gas, then attacking the VIP in his room.

- Yet another plan involved stealing hotel uniforms and infiltrating a banquet via the catering kitchen, which is always a busy and chaotic location.

Follow-up analyses by counterterrorism authorities determined that these scenarios would have carried a 90 percent success rate, and the VIP — as well as multiple protection agents — would have been killed.

In the aftermath of the New York City bomb plots, intelligence also indicated that elements associated with al Qaeda had planned to detonate car bombs at hotels where high-value targets were staying.

Determining the Threat Level

The threat to hotels is not equal around the globe, and in fact is highly correlated to geography. Geographic threat rankings are as follows:

- High. Hotels in Islamic countries with a proven level of militant activity and a regime that Islamists consider hostile, especially Iraq, Saudi Arabia, Yemen, Jordan, Turkey, Kuwait, Pakistan, the Philippines, Indonesia, Kenya, Ethiopia and Sudan. At a slightly lower level, the rest of the Persian Gulf can be included in this ranking, as can North Africa — including Morocco, Algeria, Tunisia and Egypt — and much of Central Asia. Though Israel boasts some of the world's most secure hotels, the threat level there remains quite high.

- Moderate. Hotels in other countries with a proven Islamist militant presence, especially India, Russia, Malaysia and much of Western Europe — notably Spain, Italy, France, Germany, Poland, Belgium, the Netherlands and the United Kingdom. Asian nations that are considered allies of the United States — including Japan, Singapore and South Korea, and particularly those with a rich tourism trade such as Australia and Thailand — also are included. Hotels in major U.S. cities, such as New York City, Washington, D.C., San Francisco, Los Angeles, Chicago, Atlanta, Detroit and Houston also rank in this tier. STRATFOR views Houston, New York City and Washington as particularly high-risk cities.

- Low. Hotels in Latin America are at low risk of strikes by Islamist militants. Most of Central, Eastern and Northern Europe ranks in this tier, as does China and most of North America (excepting the major U.S. cities noted above). Hotels in the United States and, to some degree, Europe, are at lower risk, due to the vast number of other soft targets — especially public transportation — available to militants.

U.S. counterterrorism sources tell STRATFOR that they are particularly concerned about hotels in two locations: Amman, Jordan, and Saudi Arabia. In Amman, the concerns center on the large Western hotel chains that serve as forward deployment locations for contractors, journalists and others waiting to enter Iraq. One hotel that is popular among Westerners is located very near the U.S. Embassy. The hotels and bars are filled with Westerners and could make attractive targets for Jordan's substantial Islamist militant community.

Sources within Saudi Arabia also have expressed concern about the large Western hotel chains, specifically because they lack basic security measures — such as standoff perimeters and ballistic window film. STRATFOR shares the view that an attack against a Western hotel in Saudi Arabia is just a matter of time.

Meanwhile, British and Australian intelligence sources cited in June 2004 by the Far Eastern Economic Review said they believe Indonesian militant group Jemaah Islamiyah (JI) has shifted its tactics away from car bombings toward targeted assassinations of Western VIPs. The report specifically mentioned the risk to British, American and Australian diplomats but also warned that JI assassins could widen their target sets to include foreign businesspeople.

Recommendations

The first step for large hotel operators in dealing with this threat is to undertake a vulnerability assessment to identify properties that are most likely to be at risk. Such an assessment — based primarily upon assets' geographic locations and an understanding of Islamist intentions and areas of operations — will allow companies to focus their time and resources on the most vulnerable properties, while more generally ensuring that security measures do not overshoot or undershoot the threat level for a particular property. This allows for better, more efficient use of resources.

For high-threat properties, the next step is usually a physical security survey to identify specific weaknesses and vulnerabilities. In some cases, diagnostic protective surveillance can help to ensure that properties are not currently under hostile surveillance. Some kind of ongoing protective surveillance program is the best insurance for interdicting hostile actions.

Because of the very large number of potential targets in most locations, the implementation of some very basic but visible measures might be sufficient to send an attacker on to the next possible target. These security enhancements include:

- Greater number and visibility of armed guards inside and outside the building.

- Prominent security cameras around the perimeter and throughout the hotel. Even if the tapes are not monitored by guards trained in countersurveillance techniques, they can help identify suspicious activity or deter hostile surveillance.

- Landscaping in front of and around the hotel that prevents vehicles from directly approaching the entrance or actually entering the building — for example, large cement flower pots that can stop vehicles, hills with rocks embedded in them, and palm trees.

Other security measures might be appropriate in medium- and high-threat level locations:

- If possible, increase the stand-off distance between the hotel and areas of vehicular traffic. Physical barricades are among the most effective deterrents to vehicle bombings, helping to keep drivers from crashing through the doors of a hotel and detonating explosives in high-traffic areas.

- In higher-threat level locations, use static surveillance around the hotel's perimeter. In areas of lesser threats, roving vehicles patrolling the perimeter at varying times might be sufficient.

The following practices also are recommended for all locations:

- Use of plastic window film throughout the hotel — it is one of the best and most cost-effective ways of minimizing casualties in the event of an attack.

- Protective surveillance. In all areas, hotel owners should consider hiring their own protective surveillance.

- Employee education. At minimum, hotels should train employees, especially doormen and other ground-level employees, in basic protective-surveillance techniques.

- Maintain a good working relationship with local police and other relevant authorities. Identifying hostile surveillance is useless unless a plan is in place to deal with it. Sound relationships with local police and other agencies — such as foreign embassies in overseas locations — are the answer. Though authorities might not be able to spare resources to monitor a hotel, in many places they will respond quickly to reports of suspected surveillance activity, confront suspicious people and possibly head off an operation.

- The ability to share guest lists with local authorities for comparison with a militant watch list could help determine if a registered guest is engaging in preoperational surveillance.

Air Marshals and Risk Mitigation
Dec. 15, 2005

U.S. media attention has again returned to the Federal Air Marshal Program, following the fatal shooting of an airline passenger on a Miami jetway last week — and fresh news, on Dec. 14, that a test of the marshal program will be run on passenger rail and bus systems in some U.S. cities. Intriguingly, the expansion plans are being made public in the wake of a 9/11 Commission report that says the government still hasn't done enough to ensure homeland security in the four years since the Sept. 11 al Qaeda attacks.

Of course, the homeland security dilemma has many aspects, and the air marshal program is only a part of one of those — transportation security. But it is a significant program, in that it touches directly on the psychological comfort (or lack thereof) of American travelers and commuters, which has direct economic impacts. Taken together, the Miami shooting, news of the marshal program's plans for expansion and the 9/11 Commission report underscore some compelling truths — and raise some deeper questions — about U.S. homeland security as a whole:

- The air marshal program, where it is in use today, is working. The shooting of an unarmed passenger in Miami, while potentially controversial for outside observers, unfolded along more-or-less textbook lines from a security perspective: A threat emerged on board an aircraft, air marshals were present to monitor and react to the threat and, once the situation exceeded a certain threshold, officers shot to kill.

While most of the post-event questions focused on whether the shooting of the passenger — who reportedly was mentally ill but was not armed — was justified, it raises a very different question from a security perspective: What would have been the outcome if the same event, or one involving a passenger who actually was carrying a weapon, had occurred on a flight that was not manned by an air marshal? Certainly, not all U.S. flights have security coverage, and there is potential for loopholes to be exploited.

- The U.S. government clearly recognizes the vulnerabilities of the public transportation system, which Islamist militants — even prior to what is recognized as al Qaeda today — have a long history of targeting. And while plans to protect passenger rail systems are important, the evolution of a protective strategy has been slow. The plan announced Dec. 14 has certain merits and drawbacks, but the diversion of scarce resources from the airline industry to other forms of transportation would not, on its face, appear to be the wisest solution to the security problem.

Having said that, the diversion of air marshals may in fact be the most viable fix to the dilemma, at least for the near term. In what could be termed the federal "war for funding," the proposal announced Dec. 14 — in which air marshals would team up with local police or transit authority security forces to monitor threats on subways and buses in certain cities — was

63

a shrewd move by the Transportation Security Administration (TSA). Not only is it responding to congressional pressure to do more for national security, it is also highlighting its capabilities in a way that eventually could lead to greater funding for the air marshal program, which has been operating at a manpower deficit from the beginning.

The issue with which the TSA is struggling is the classic dilemma of a growing business in any competitive industry: At a certain point, it often becomes necessary to expand operations or areas of focus in order to grow (in terms of manpower and revenue). With the Dec. 14 announcement, it appears that the air marshals are surging forward to fill an obvious vacuum in the U.S. security infrastructure in a way that few, if any, other federal security agencies could.

Applied on a limited basis — as the upcoming rail-security test has been devised — this is a move that could yield important insights and developments in protecting public transportation systems. But there also is a clear risk that the TSA's ability to protect, with a fixed number of assets, both commercial aircraft and other forms of transportation could be affected.

To be sure, neither the TSA nor the air marshals have yet mastered all the intricacies of protecting commercial air flights, as the 9/11 Commission recently pointed out. In all fairness, the problems in that area are not issues that any government agency can overcome on its own. They are combinations of manpower shortages, bureaucratic inefficiencies, commercial considerations and — let's face it — political will on the part of the public.

It is easy to cite the flaws in the U.S. air-travel security program — and some international security leaders are fond of doing so — when it is compared to a leading industry example: Israel's El Al airline. In this case, the numbers alone tell much of the story: El Al receives comprehensive security coverage for each of its 31 aircraft, which fly into and out of a single airport (Ben Gurion) with an annual passenger load of just over 3 million people, according to 2004 figures. In the United States, the eight largest commercial carriers own a combined 2,861 aircraft, which fly in and out of dozens of airports on a regular basis, with a 2004 passenger load of more than 483.7 million people.

In El Al's case, two to four Shin Bet agents accompany each flight, and crew members —who frequently are veterans of the Israeli Defense Forces — have security training as well. The precise number of U.S. federal air marshals working today is not known, but officials say it now numbers in the "thousands," as opposed to about three dozen at the time of the Sept. 11 attacks. However, there is a gap between the number of assets available and the number of flights demanding protection — thus, many flights go without federal protection, and civilian crew members cannot necessarily fill the void.

There are other differences as well, many of them structurally driven. For instance, El Al's pre-flight screening procures are detailed and intensive, with each passenger subjected to covert surveillance and interviewed about travel histories before ever boarding a flight. There is a public/private partnership at work behind the scenes: Because El Al is a state-owned airline — and that state considers itself to be perpetually at war — there is an unwavering commitment to security; protective systems have been hard-wired into its business methods, and revenue and profit considerations take a lower priority. In the United States, attention to airline security (indeed, all forms of travel security) has been reactive rather than pre-emptive, and attempts to fuse security considerations into business methods frequently come into direct and predictable conflict with profit and revenue considerations.

In short, it is not possible, in the United States, to simply "protect things the Israeli way," as some have suggested, because of the vast differences in scale and the fundamental structural differences between not only the airline industries but also government and public mindsets.

Given those limitations, the TSA has been using what, to our minds, is the most logical means of deploying limited assets: It uses a "threat matrix" that combines known information about threatening groups with, when possible, intelligence about direct threats or risks to specific areas. For instance, a commercial flight from London to New York City or from Damascus to Washington, D.C., likely would be manned by an air marshal as a way of mitigating threats from al Qaeda or other Islamist groups, whereas an internal flight from Columbus, Ohio, to Charleston, W. Va., would not — unless, for example, security agencies were to get a tip about a plot touching on those areas in some way. This is, as we say, a logical method, but not a foolproof one, as there have been instances when some high-risk flights had no marshal coverage at all.

Any search for a perfect solution would, in the end, be a vain one. It might be possible for El Al to provide flawless security aboard its aircraft, but Israelis standing in line at bus stops in some cities are risking life and limb. Likewise, the only truly viable security systems to be found in the U.S. context are those striving for risk management and deterrence, rather than total risk elimination. This will be a permanent feature of the U.S. travel industry — whether applied to airlines, commuter rail or public bus systems.

It is against this backdrop that the expansion of the program — even on a test basis — to rail and bus systems becomes interesting. Security in other areas of transportation, particularly passenger rail, is indeed needed. In the wake of the July 7 attacks in London, the Madrid bombings nearly two years ago, and ongoing — albeit intermittent — rumors and threats of terrorist attacks within the United States, doing nothing to protect the rail systems is not, for the Bush administration, an option. For the TSA, having the air marshals step up to lend a hand in this area could, in time, bring in more funding to help plug holes in the existing system as well.

But at the same time, disturbing questions about the speed of the federal government's response still linger. Threats to passenger-rail systems have not been as clearly visible in the United States as threats to commercial airliners, but they have been visible in the global context for quite some time, and passenger rail was pinpointed as a vulnerability even before the Madrid attacks took place. Further, the learning curve of terrorist groups — including but not limited to al Qaeda — has been material for considerable study; groups in various parts of the world learn from each other and can adapt techniques and methods used elsewhere quite easily. But the learning curve — measured by response — for the U.S. government is not as dynamic. While the nation's pre-emptive intelligence efforts have improved, protective security responses still are coming late.

Self-Preservation Techniques for Airline Passengers
Jan. 13, 2006

The International Air Transport Association, a Montreal-based industry group, predicts the number of people who fly each year on business and leisure will soon top 2 billion worldwide. As traffic rises, airports around the world are increasingly jammed with crowds of passengers waiting to check in, pass security and board their flights. Although the congestion increases pressure on security authorities, the fact is that air travel is safer today — in the post-Sept. 11 environment — than it has been in years. Passengers, however, should not rely solely on outside security for their personal protection.

Air marshals are present on U.S. and many foreign airlines, cockpit doors remain locked while the plane is in flight and international "no-fly" databases are aimed at ensuring that people who pose a potential threat do not board international flights. Perhaps most effective is the heightened state of vigilance and awareness that air travelers have adopted since the Sept. 11 attacks. In addition to official security, hijackers also would have to contend with a plane full of passengers who know now that the highjacking could be a suicide mission — and that their lives are at stake.

Even with this atmosphere of security surrounding air travel, travelers nevertheless can take steps to ensure their own security while on a plane. Passengers who include a smoke hood and a small flashlight among their carry-on items, for example, could help themselves in an emergency situation, whether it be an attack or an accident aboard the aircraft. In such situations, smoke inhalation, especially from the extremely toxic burning plastics within a plane, poses a serious threat. In addition, a flashlight can be used to facilitate getting off of the aircraft when the power is out and the air is thick with smoke.

With more emphasis placed on securing aircraft, however, militants could be content to confine their attacks to terminals, where crowds of waiting people present an enticing target for militants aiming to cause mass casualties. Travelers, however, can mitigate the risks by maintaining a high degree of situational awareness and taking other personal protection measures.

In a security sense, airport terminals are divided into two parts. The "soft side" is before the security checkpoint — where passengers and carry-on luggage is screened — while the "hard side" is after. Time spent in line at the ticket counter and then at security checkpoints, therefore, should be minimized. In the first case, arriving at the counter early enough to avoid the mad dash of latecomers would help, while avoiding wearing clothes with lots of metal buttons and buckles, and minimizing carry-on baggage can expedite getting through security. Once on the hard side, travelers should avoid the waiting areas at the gate, if possible, by utilizing the members-only lounges operated by many airlines. This helps to keep the traveler out of a potential attack zone — away from crowds and out of plain view.

In many parts of the world, air travel can be dangerous because of lax maintenance and safety procedures. This is especially true in the developing world, where maintenance regulations and procedures often are not strictly enforced. The U.S. Federal Aviation Administration prohibits U.S. carriers from flying into foreign airports that do not meet security and safety standards. Although this information is not readily available to the public, determined travelers could contact the FAA for a list — and then avoid those airlines and airports that U.S. authorities consider substandard. The consular information sheets issued by the U.S. State Department also provide information about air travel safety.

At the destination airport, transportation can be arranged in advance to further minimize time spent on the soft side. For traveling executives, discretion should be employed when it comes to finding the local driver on the other end of a flight. A driver who holds up a sign bearing the executive's name and/or the company's name could tip off potential kidnappers and terrorists to the presence of a high-value target.

Airport terminals, especially in the developing world, are notorious for criminal activity. When on the soft side, unattended luggage can be stolen and travelers can be victimized by pickpockets — especially when they are less vigilant after a long, exhausting intercontinental flight.

Situational awareness and preparation are the most effective personal security measures a traveler can take.

Paying attention to people and events in the area and avoiding potential attack zones are two basics for self-preservation while in the terminal and on the plane.

The Risks of Public Transportation
Jan. 20, 2006

Travelers who rely on public transportation in some parts of the world risk losing their wallets or purses — if not their lives — to criminal or terrorist elements. Recent history has shown that buses, taxis and even subways can be extremely dangerous. When at all possible, travelers are better off using private transportation, or at least exercising the utmost caution while even in the vicinity of public transportation vehicles or facilities — as the Jan. 19 suicide bombing near the Old Central Bus Station in Tel Aviv, Israel, proved.

By far, the most common threat to passengers on buses and at bus stations are petty crimes such as pickpocketing. But bus stations and the buses also make excellent terrorist targets. Although Tel Aviv's Old Central Bus Station apparently was not the main site of the Jan. 19 attack, three previous attacks have occurred in the vicinity since 2000. In Baghdad, bus stations also are frequently targeted by suicide bombers. Buses are one of the favored militant targets because they present not only the opportunity to kill or maim a large number of people, but also because they allow the bomber to target a specific demographic group, such as Shia heading to a shrine south of Baghdad or

Israeli soldiers waiting at a bus station in Tel Aviv. These are basic targeting criteria for militants.

Taxis also present a significant degree of risk in many countries, where visitors have been robbed or abducted while in a taxi from the local airport or while riding around city streets. In many cases, taxi drivers actually belong to criminal gangs who use the driver to deliver unwitting passengers to armed accomplices waiting nearby. From there, the visitor can become the victim of an "express kidnapping," in which he is forced to withdraw money from his bank account using his ATM card. In other scenarios, the driver might fake having engine problems or simply stop at a traffic light to give accomplices in a following car an opportunity to enter the cab and rob the passenger.

In cities such as Mexico City and Bogota, Colombia, foreigners should never hail a taxi on the street and should never share a cab with a person other than the driver, including the driver's so-called "brother," "son" or "cousin," who are often preludes to a criminal attack. Furthermore, taxis are not well regulated in many cities, which means "independent" drivers — some not using taxi meters — roam around the streets looking for potential passengers. In parts of the former Soviet Union, including Moscow, people hailing a taxi have had private cars stop to offer rides. In most of the world's more developed countries it is against the law to ride in a taxi that is not accredited or certified by the government — and those who do so put themselves at risk not only of falling victim to crime but also of being caught in illegal activities.

In India, authorities have taken steps to safeguard cab riders — and preserve the country's tourism industry —

following attacks against passengers, including the rape and killing of a female Australian tourist by a New Delhi taxi driver in March 2004. In addition, the Indian Tourism Ministry established a special taxi service for women. Of course, this is no guarantee that all taxis in the country are safe.

In China, on the other hand, the Beijing airport operates regulated and well-secured taxi lines, and the taxi companies provide a card and pamphlet (in poor English) with phone numbers to call if the service is unsatisfactory.

In many cities worldwide, international travelers often prefer to use the subway or metro system, finding it cheaper, faster, less language-dependent and more reliable than taxis or buses. The threat of petty crime and terrorist attack, however, is no less significant with this mode of transportation. To mitigate these threats, hiring a private car service often is the best way to go — and reputable cars for hire can be reserved in advance through hotels or reliable local sources. Many hotels also have exclusive arrangements with accredited taxi companies.

In many cities, especially ones in the developing world, business visitors often are met at the airport by company vehicles with drivers who sometimes double as armed security escorts. As a precaution, waiting drivers should not hold out a sign with the passenger or company's name at the airport, as it could attract kidnappers or extortionists who know companies will pay ransoms.

Detailed and customized information about specific threats to travelers overseas can be obtained by utilizing a private security consulting firm. In addition, consular information sheets provided by the U.S. State Department and similar services provided by the British and Australian foreign ministries list common crime and/or transportation problems for particular countries.

Protecting Information in Electronic Devices
Jan. 27, 2006

The tag line of an old American Express commercial warned travelers, "Don't leave home without it." In today's world, the business traveler finds it hard to leave home without at least a laptop, cell phone and personal data assistant (PDA). Some also tote iPods in which sensitive information has been stored. Executives who fail to secure these devices while traveling abroad, however, are exposing the information they contain to the possibility of theft from business competitors — and even from foreign governments.

Criminals, too, like laptops because of their high value on the resale market. These devices are frequently stolen in airports, bars and restaurants and on trains, buses and even the street. Therefore, a laptop should not be set down in a place where a thief can quickly snatch it and run. In addition, it is a good idea to carry a laptop in a non-typical bag, rather than its case, which often has the manufacturer's logo on it.

Beyond the risk of a snatch-and-run robbery, however, is the chance that private business competitors or foreign governments — or state-owned or -operated business competitors — will peek into the system in order to glean valuable company-specific information such as client lists and account numbers.

Some countries have been known to use their national intelligence services to spy on visiting executives, especially when the executive's competition is state-subsidized. This makes the visitor's information vulnerable not only to hostile intelligence but also to hostile intelligence backed by the resources of a government, which is a significantly greater threat than corporate spies. This has been known to occur in Russia, India and China, as well as in countries that many executives would not consider hostile in this area, such as France and Israel.

Using a commercially available encryption program can help protect sensitive information on computers when traveling. To further safeguard the information, however, the program's pass code should never be cached in the computer's memory. In addition, icons for the encryption program should not be displayed on the desktop or taskbar. In some countries, airport security personnel have been known to start up a visiting executive's laptop and, upon finding a software encryption program icon, attempt to retrieve the computer's data. In some countries, laptop screens have been smashed by frustrated intelligence officers who have discovered that the device was password-protected and encrypted.

The best way to protect sensitive information contained in a laptop or PDA is to avoid exposing the device to potentially compromising situations. Minimizing the amount of sensitive information stored on the computer also is a good idea. In other words, the computer should contain only information that is specific to the current trip and, when possible, it should not contain account numbers, passwords or other sensitive information. Then, should the device be compromised, the executive can take some small comfort in knowing that not all of the company's sensitive information has leaked out. It goes without saying that no sensitive information should be stored on cell phones or iPods, especially when traveling abroad.

It also is important to ensure that all important data on a laptop is backed up in another location. In high-crime areas it is advisable to carry the laptop's hard drive separately from the rest of the computer, such as in a coat pocket. Then, should the laptop be stolen, the thief will not get the data — which likely is much more valuable to a traveling executive than the machine itself.

In some countries, it is not beyond the local intelligence service to steal a visiting executive's laptop and make it look like a simple theft. For this reason, a laptop should never be left in a hotel room or even in the room's safe — especially in a country in which the government has only to ask the hotel for the pass key to get in.

Because of this, ensuring constant, physical security of PDAs and laptops is one way to have the best chance of securing important information. Executive protection personnel should take custody of a traveling executive's PDA and/or laptop when they are not being used; while the executive is making a speech or attending dinners or other engagements, for example.

Another way to avoid exposing a laptop to a security breach is to leave the laptop at home and instead carry a device such as a BlackBerry or other PDA. These devices are small enough to tuck inside a pocket and thus can be carried at all times. Of course, this does not eliminate the theft risk — and wireless devices carry their own inherent security risks — but at least the devices can be kept close at hand.

Laptops and other electronic devices have become essential travel accessories because of the vast amount of information they can hold in a relatively small space. For the same reason, they also make a prize catch for anyone with hostile intentions. Travelers who take precautions to safeguard the information on these devices and to mitigate the potential adverse effects of a compromise could be saving their companies from serious harm.

Common-Sense Measures for Leisure Time
Jan. 31, 2006

Westerners who travel abroad on business often find they must entertain themselves in the evenings or during breaks between meetings. Some even build extra time into their schedules in order to become better acquainted with their host city. These times, however, can be especially risky for strangers in a strange land.

In many countries the number of people who should not be trusted generally exceeds those who can. Included in this list are many the Western traveler would not normally suspect of having hostile intentions, such as taxi drivers, street vendors, those claiming to offer guide services, prostitutes — and even law enforcement officials and children.

Westerners, and particularly U.S. citizens, often are targeted for robbery or kidnappings — at the hands of common criminals or militant groups — simply because they are believed to have deep pockets. They must remain vigilant against possible threats to their personal security, especially after business hours, when people tend to let their guard down.

Bars and casinos represent a threat for many reasons, especially those venues that might cater to prostitutes or drug traffickers. A traveling executive who engages in some form of illicit liaison can find one or more of his or her companion's accomplices lying in wait to commit a robbery — or worse.

In many countries, taxi drivers often are part-time criminals. Some will offer to take visitors to a local hot spot off the beaten path when they are actuality setting the visitors up for robbery. Street vendors also can make a victim out of an unwitting visitor by offering to escort the foreigner someplace to look at merchandise or to meet local artisans. These scenarios sometimes end in a bad part of town where accomplices are waiting to commit robbery or cause bodily harm.

Children are known to be expert pickpockets in many countries, and they often will surround a traveling Westerner, seemingly to talk or ask questions but in reality to remove his or her possessions.

Although there have been stories of Western visitors breaking local laws and getting off with only a fine or a "slap on the wrist," foreigners who engage in illegal activity while abroad can find themselves in serious trouble. First, taking part in unregulated, illegal activities such as gambling, prostitution, drug transactions or black-marketeering puts the visitor in contact with a criminal element, which can lead to violence. Second, in many countries, local law enforcement officials literally have the power of life and death over people who break the law in their jurisdictions. They can be just as likely as a criminal element to beat, rob or even kill someone in their custody. Before departing, it is a good idea to be absolutely clear on the destination country's laws.

Criminal elements also will take advantage of a visitor's lack of familiarity with local geography and customs. Travelers who walk around a foreign city with the idea of taking in the local color risk wandering into a dangerous neighborhood. Just as in the United States, foreign cities have areas that are dangerous for local inhabitants, to say nothing of conspicuous strangers. This risk is compounded when the wandering occurs at night, even when travelers are in a small group.

In order to keep a low profile, visitors should dress conservatively, especially in a conservative or religious country. They also should avoid wearing clothing purchased locally, as they can miss the subtle meaning of a color or pattern — and perhaps offend the wrong people.

The desire to record travel memories on videotape or photos also can lead to problems for travelers who are unaware of local laws and customs. In many countries it is forbidden to photograph military installations or government buildings. Security forces also can take offense when being photographed and in some parts of the world may respond by confiscating film, breaking cameras or worse. It also can be dangerous to photograph civilians, as in many countries this is considered offensive behavior. This goes doubly for locals

79

taking part in religious rituals, as they can react negatively, perhaps aggressively, to having their pictures taken, or even to being asked to be photographed by an outsider.

To avoid having trouble abroad, traveling executives should use common sense and always maintain a high state of situational awareness. The same general rules that apply in any large U.S. city also apply in cities around the world: Avoid hustlers, muggers, gangsters, pimps, grifters and pushers. In many parts of the world, however, these elements are more prolific and brazen than in U.S. cities.

When preparing for a trip abroad, travelers should consult the U.S. State Department's consular information sheet on the destination country. This document, as well as any recent Warden Message, will contain information on potential threats and recent trends in local criminal activity. For more information about generally safe places to visit — and those to avoid — the concierge in most quality hotels can be a reliable, knowledgeable guide. In some cities, however, it could be advisable not to leave the hotel at all during leisure times. By staying in the hotel and taking advantage of the services in the resident bar or restaurant, the visitor minimizes contact with potential criminal elements. Furthermore, by charging meals and drinks to the room, travelers avoid having to carry a large amount of cash.

Westerners who want to avoid danger while traveling abroad will arrive in their host country with a basic knowledge of local threats, laws and customs. Furthermore, they will avoid danger zones and maintain situational awareness at all times. Practicing a little common sense can't hurt either.

Residential Security: Assessing the Environment
March 8, 2006

A common bond among people throughout the world, regardless of nationality or place of residence, is the need to feel safe in one's home and to protect the family members who dwell in it from criminal invasion and other threats. In some neighborhoods in the United States and elsewhere, security might mean simply locking the front door at night and turning on the porch light. In many other places, residential security can be much more complicated. In all cases, having a plan for residential security is of key importance.

Effective residential security planning starts from the outside and works in. This allows residents and security professionals to make informed choices, beginning with the selection of a residence location, and down to detailed decisions about guards, fences, locks and alarms. Both limitations on resources and aesthetic considerations call for a measured, informed approach to security countermeasures.

The first step, then, is to assess the general security environment of the region in which one lives, taking into account both the national and city-specific history of crime, terrorism and civil unrest — and the current climate on all three. Residential security should be more robust in Beirut, Lebanon, for example, than in Oslo, Norway. The potential threat from natural disasters such as floods, earthquakes and hurricanes also should be taken into account, as should the threat of martial law or government-imposed curfews that could leave residents isolated and, perhaps, without basic supplies and services. In such environments, a good security

81

plan will provide for self-sufficiency in case of infrastructure disruptions and imposed limitations on mobility.

The next steps are assessments of the specific security environment of the neighborhood and of the strengths and vulnerabilities of the residence itself. It also is vital to understand whether the inhabitants themselves are prime targets for crime or terrorism simply because of their nationality, job position or level of wealth. Western housing compounds in some countries can be particularly vulnerable to terrorist attack, for example, because of their symbolic value and the likelihood that a strike would cause a high number of casualties. Similarly, the occupants of the home of a high-profile executive or government official might be more attractive to kidnappers or other criminals because of the wealth or status associated with the person's job. Entire neighborhoods, in fact, can be targeted by professional criminals because of their affluence. Of course, the number of valuables inside the home also increases the risk factor. A person with a multi-million-dollar art collection has a greater chance of being targeted by art thieves than someone without such a collection, for instance.

The effectiveness of local law enforcement and emergency response personnel also should be evaluated. If something goes wrong, what are the chances of getting help from them? Law enforcement that tends to respond ineffectively to petty crime often is opening the door to criminals of all kinds, including violent ones. If possible, a statistical history of crime in the neighborhood, usually available from local law enforcement, should be studied. Questions to be answered include: Are violent or confrontational crimes prevalent, as opposed to petty theft?

Are home invasions common? It should be borne in mind that in many areas (Mexico City, for example), serious crimes often go unreported, due to mistrust of the police and lack of public confidence in their competence. In such cases, official government statistics are not to be trusted, and a deeper, perhaps more intuitive, study is required.

Whether one lives in an urban or rural setting is another consideration when determining to what degree the home must be secured and the kind of contingency plan to put in place. Recovering from a disaster, violent crime or militant attack could be more difficult in a remote area or a town with poorly developed facilities. With this in mind, an assessment of the area's infrastructure should be made, with attention paid to the availability and reliability of communications and electricity as well as the quality of local medical facilities. The specific questions when considering this issue would include: Should the residence have backup generators in case of power loss? Is a secondary supply of food and drinking water needed? How far away is the nearest hospital? What are its standards of treatment and equipment?

Beyond the safeguards that might be needed for a particular dwelling, it also is important to know the risks associated with the geography of the immediate neighborhood. Some street layouts, for example, are attractive to criminals and potential attackers because they offer easy access to the neighborhood from outside or rapid escape routes after crimes have been committed. Some neighborhoods include features such as trees and bushes, vacant lots, or busy roads that help those engaged in hostile surveillance blend in. Local ordinances or covenants that restrict the erection or walls or the use of security measures such as window grates or certain lighting also can be a factor in determining the security of a neighborhood. In addition to examining the immediate vicinity, the surrounding areas also should be evaluated for their level of crime or other hostile activity, as these problems can easily spill over and become a direct security threat.

Once the broader security analysis is complete, residents can begin to create an informed plan to protect their home and its occupants.

The Five Rings of Protection
March 9, 2006

The "outside-in" approach to developing an effective residential security plan involves a system of five concentric rings of protection. The outermost ring is off the property in the area surrounding the residence. The second ring usually is the residence property line, and the third is the outer perimeter and grounds. The fourth ring is the "hard line," the actual walls of the residence, and the final, innermost circle is the safe haven, a place to shelter during an attack or intrusion.

Ideally, a professional security service that is trained in countersurveillance should provide the first ring of protection, by patrolling the neighborhood regularly. In U.S. neighborhoods, however, this function often is performed by police and neighborhood watch programs, both of which can be effective deterrents to crime. If dedicated security patrols are not available, residents should encourage local authorities to step up police patrols and develop a cooperative relationship with others in the vicinity. The area around the residence also should be well-lighted at night to discourage both surveillance and criminal activity.

The second ring starts with a clearly delineated property line, which is marked as private property and includes physical barriers such as fences or hedges to discourage casual or accidental intrusion. For this, aesthetic considerations should be taken into account. A high wall topped with razor wire, for example, might not fit in with many residential areas. If possible, the entire property line should be accessible to security personnel, including police, so that they can regularly inspect the entire perimeter to watch for signs of intrusion.

Depending on the size of the area contained by the property line and the available security personnel, the outer perimeter of the property — the third ring — can reach to the property line. For larger estates, however, fencing in the entire property might not be feasible, meaning the outer perimeter will be closer in to the residence. In general, it is better to establish an outer perimeter that can be adequately patrolled and protected by available security personnel than to try to cover too much area and have security spread thin. In any case, the outer perimeter should, at a minimum, provide a physical barrier to intrusion and shield the property from prying eyes such as paparazzi or hostile surveillance. The physical barrier along the outer perimeter can range from aesthetically pleasing privacy fencing or hedges to electric fencing or massive concrete walls topped by razor wire.

If the security assessment has deemed it necessary, the outer perimeter also can be monitored by security personnel and/or the resident using closed-circuit television cameras. The perimeter should be well-lighted to discourage intruders and to provide enough light for the cameras to be effective. Where aesthetic concerns or local light-pollution ordinances must be considered, infrared lighting and infrared sensitive cameras can be used. Intrusion-detection equipment, such as pressure plates, buried radio frequency loops or motion-detector systems — all connected to alarms — also can be used.

Full lighting should be available on demand, in case of emergency, though suddenly flooding the grounds with light can be a double-edged sword: It can expose intruders, but it also can reveal the location of residents and/or security personnel. Therefore, the circumstances and techniques for employing full lighting should be carefully considered, based on the situation.

The outer perimeter should be established far enough away from the residence to provide enough stand-off distance to mitigate the effects of explosives or to give security personnel a better chance of intercepting an intruder who is heading for the house. In extreme cases, in regions in which the overall threat is especially pronounced or the resident is assessed to be at extreme risk, the outer perimeter should be actively patrolled at all times by human security personnel. These can include armed or unarmed security guards, on foot or in patrol vehicles. Guard dogs can be employed in extreme situations, as they make excellent patrol and detection assets, especially with an armed handler.

In some cases, an upper-floor apartment in a well-secured building can be a wise choice for housing because such living provides a degree of anonymity, while access to the public is limited via the use of security cards or doormen. However, the quality of the building's security system and personnel, as well as the risk incurred by living in close proximity to the other residents, some of whom may be high-value-targets, must be taken into consideration. Apartment living also complicates fire/evacuation plans.

The dwelling's grounds, part of the third ring of security, also can be covered by closed-circuit TV or seismic detection devices, infrared cameras and motion detectors. Any system, however, should be linked to a single, integrated alarm set to alert both security personnel and residents to any intrusion.

Residents and security management should develop clear understandings with first responders, such as local police, as to the actions they will take should an intrusion occur beyond the outer perimeter. These procedures should be tested by both residents and security personnel, with response times carefully noted.

The "hard line" — the walls, doors and windows of the residence itself — makes up the fourth ring. In practical and legal terms, this barrier can and should be protected according to the level deemed appropriate in the overall security assessment and, if necessary, defended with force. The hard line should have its own system of passive and active defenses. Passive defenses include robust construction, locks, landscape features and security procedures, while active defenses include alarms, detection systems and security personnel.

Special attention should be paid to the strength, quality and proper installation of doors and locks. Ideally, cipher locks with combinations that can be changed frequently should be used, as changing the combinations mitigates the threat of a former, possibly disgruntled, employee or staffer from having access to sensitive areas. In cases in which a combination lock is not optimal, a good quality dead bolt also can be effective. Double-cylinder dead bolts should be used if the door is near any window. Both types of locks can be augmented by a simple slide bolt that goes into the floor. In all cases, locks should be professionally selected and installed by specialists. However, the best lock in the world, even when set in a sturdy metal door, can easily be kicked in if it also extends into a cheap wood frame.

Special attention should be paid to windows, especially ground-floor windows. It goes without saying that locks on ordinary glass windows are useless, as shattering or removing a glass pane allows access to the residence. In extreme cases, then, ground-floor windows should be barred, as should any higher window that can be reached if the intruder climbs onto a wall or tree. Of course, emergency releases should be installed on an adequate number of the window bars to allow for escape in case of fire. Wherever possible, landscaping features such as hedges should be kept away from hard-line walls, windows and doors, as they can conceal an intruder. Another passive defense is having the entire hard line flooded with light, infrared if necessary. In addition, any outside roof access ladders should be enclosed by cages and locked.

Active defenses along the hard line should consist of redundant intrusion-detection systems and individual alarms that are connected to the overall alarm system but that function if the main system fails. The system should be backed up with battery power in case electric power is lost or disconnected. A cell phone backup also should be at hand at all times, in case the phone lines go down or are cut. In addition, door and window alarms plus systems that detect motion or glass breakage can be installed inside the residence if the broader assessment demands their use.

"Panic alarms," those that can alert the entire household and even local police to an intrusion, also should be discreetly placed in several strategic locations around the residence. And an intrusion beyond the hard line must always be treated as an extreme emergency until security responders can clear the residence. This requires that security respond immediately and aggressively to an intrusion and that the residents retire immediately to the final ring of protection — the safe-haven.

It is important to note that a security plan should be commensurate with the overall threat assessment for the residence. In other words, while the five rings of protection are standard for every dwelling, the degree to which they are reinforced can fluctuate. What works to prevent criminal intrusion may not be sufficient to defend against militant attackers armed with heavy weapons or explosives. Also, some individuals, based on their status or what they symbolize, are at greater risk than others and require fuller security. With this in mind, a measured response to the assessed threats should be applied.

Safe Havens and Evacuation Plans
March 9, 2006

Of the five rings of protection in residential security, the innermost ring is the safe haven, or "panic room." It is the place to which residents can retreat if a potentially violent intruder successfully penetrates the outer security rings and gains entry into the residence.

Safe havens are small, windowless rooms such as sufficiently sized and unobstructed closets or purpose-built rooms designed and installed by professionals. In most cases, using these rooms is preferable to attempting to run from the residence in the event of a break-in, as running could expose the residents to the intruders.

Not all residential security plans require a safe haven, although if the decision to create or install one is part of the broader security assessment, it should become an integral part of the plan. Every home, however, should have a fire/evacuation plan.

The safe haven should be centrally located on the sleeping floor, the part of the residence where bedrooms are located. If there is more than one sleeping floor or area, each one should have its own safe haven. The pathways from the sleeping quarters to the safe haven should be easy to maneuver and free from obstructions — and they must not cross the paths likely to be used by the intruders.

Safe havens usually are rated based on the time it would take an intruder equipped with hand tools such as sledge hammers and crowbars to break into them. Thus there are 10-minute safe havens, two-hour safe havens, etc. This rating is reflected in the design and materials used in constructing the haven. The level of protection required should be based on the overall security assessment, and as a rule should at minimum protect residents for twice the known and tested average response time of security responders. In its design phase, attention should also be given to the safe haven's air supply.

The safe-haven also can be equipped with a firearm for defense, although the decision to maintain firearms for self-defense in the home is personal and specific to each family, and depends on the capabilities of family members who might use them. In the hands of a well-trained person who has the will — not everyone does — to use deadly force in an emergency, a firearm can be an effective deterrent to violent intruders. Whatever the decision, firearms must be well maintained mechanically, able to be deployed quickly under high-stress conditions and carefully secured inside the safe haven. A firearm in the hands of an untrained person is more dangerous to him or her than it is to the attacker.

As part of their attack, intruders could cut telephone and power lines. Thus, it is best to have two communication options in the safe haven in case one system is unavailable or nonfunctioning. A regular hard-line phone supplemented by a combination cell phone/radio on a battery charger would work in this case. A panic alarm whose signal is different from those of other alarms in the house also should be part of the safe haven's equipment, in order to let first responders and security personnel know that the family has gone to the safe haven. A stand-alone backup power source is advisable in case the primary power source is cut.

The safe haven should also be stocked with materials and supplies that the residents might need during an assault and subsequent siege. This includes first-aid supplies as well as necessary medications. In certain cases, the safe haven might include an inhaler for an asthma sufferer, a defibrillator for an elderly family member or insulin and sugar sources for diabetics. Auxiliary light sources such as flashlights or battery-powered lanterns will be needed if all sources of power have been interrupted. In addition, drinking water, an emergency food supply such as energy bars, and provision for toilet functions should be included in the event of a prolonged siege.

Like any security precautions, a safe haven is useless without a plan, and a plan is useless unless it is practiced. A typical plan might go as follows: When an unauthorized intrusion is detected, family members move immediately toward the safe haven. As they move, the nearest available panic alarm is activated. Once the family goes into the safe haven and secures the door, the safe-haven's alarm is activated. Then a head count is taken to ensure that everyone in the household is present. In the case of separate safe havens, the head count can be completed by phone.

During the emergency, a line of communication is established with security personnel and first responders who are briefed on the situation. It is essential that this line be kept open. The family stays inside the safe haven until the all-clear is given by security responders. This plan should be practiced by all family members in conjunction with any employed security personnel. Everyone should know the plan and their part in it so they will know what to do in the event of an emergency.

Because fire or other environmental dangers, such as gas leaks, smoke and dangerous fumes, are far more common than invasion by hostile intruders, a fire/evacuation plan should be included in every residential security plan. It is advisable to cooperate with firefighting professionals in formulating fire/evacuation plans. In many cases, experts from the local fire company are available to provide on-site advice and surveys, and some have formal training programs established, as do some home insurance carriers. In the United States, a good fire plan will at minimum adhere to standards established by National Fire Protection Association (NFPA), which provides codes for fire detection equipment. In homes with valuable art collections, some insurance carriers may impose requirements over and above those of the NFPA.

A good fire plan includes frequent, regular maintenance of detection equipment and fire extinguishers, and all adult family members should be trained in the use of extinguishers. Because kitchen fires are perhaps more common than any other kind in modern houses, consider equipping kitchens with automatic extinguishing systems employing Argonite or FM-200. If the residence contains any appliance that could produce carbon monoxide (CO), CO detectors should be installed. Obviously, these fire and smoke alarm systems should have audible tones that are easily distinguishable from intrusion alarms. Heat detectors are available for areas in the home where smoke detectors might produce false alarms.

In general, the best plan in case of fire is to evacuate the premises and leave fighting it to the professionals. A family fire plan should, at a minimum, include several evacuation options, and a single "rally point" well away from the building, where a head count can be conducted.

When formulating the evacuation plan, provision must be made for family members who have mobility problems. One or two commercially available folding escape ladders can be kept on the upper floors within easy reach of established escape routes, such as windows or balconies, in order to facilitate escape. In addition, every family member should have a commercially available smoke hood stored in or near their sleeping quarters.

The fire plan, like the security plan, must be practiced by residents and any security personnel employed. Each family member should know where to go and what to do in case of a fire. In particular, because of the physical considerations involved, the use of ladders and smoke hoods must be practiced.

When formulating an emergency action plan, it should be kept in mind that the more complex a plan is, the more likely it will fail. Plans must be simple, not only because children often must participate, but because sudden stress impairs memory and thought processes for people of all ages.

CHAPTER 4: Kidnapping

Taking Advantage of Panic
April 5, 2006

Although kidnap-for-ransom schemes, especially those involving high-profile figures, can net huge payoffs in terms of money and media exposure, creative criminals in many parts of the world have devised a way to avoid the risky and labor-intensive work of actually abducting their victims by staging so-called "virtual" kidnappings. This relatively new trend involves no abduction whatsoever. Virtual kidnappers must simply convince a target's family that a kidnapping has occurred. Though the "victim" most likely is in no danger, the panicked family members will quickly pay the "ransom" — and the virtual kidnappers will be gone before the family comes to its senses.

Virtual kidnappings rely heavily on obtaining — and exploiting — personal information about the target. In one such scheme, the kidnappers position themselves at a mall or other youth hangout claiming to offer young people a chance to enter a contest for prizes such as iPods or X-Boxes. The youths then fill out "entry blanks," unwittingly offering up personal information such as addresses, home phone numbers and the names of parents. Afterward, the kidnappers follow the potential target until he or she enters a place where cell phones cannot be immediately answered, such as a school or a movie theatre. This provides the kidnappers with a window of opportunity to call the target's parents, claim that they have abducted their child, describe details of authenticity such as what the person is wearing or where he was going, and demand that a ransom be paid immediately.

This new form of pseudo-abduction is based largely on psychological shock, scaring the victim's family into making an irrational, impulsive decision such as transferring large sums of money. The advantage to the pseudo-abductor is that none of the traditional infrastructure is required.

Typical kidnappings involve the housing and feeding of the victim, and usually require a gang of accomplices to successfully execute. With increased manpower and infrastructure, the risk grows of a kidnapping going bad. A virtual kidnapping can be pulled off by a single person or small gang, using a cell phone and requesting ransom money be deposited into an anonymous bank account.

This is a very quick process compared to conventional kidnappings, which can take several weeks to negotiate a release. Virtual kidnappings rely on the element of surprise and a demand for ransom within the hour, giving no time for the family to consider their options or contact authorities. In the event virtual kidnappers are caught, they do not face the same punishments as conventional kidnappers. A virtual kidnapping essentially is extortion, with no physical harm coming to anyone.

While virtual kidnappings have not been widely seen in the United States, they have become more common in countries with dense urban populations like Taiwan, Mexico and Brazil. In Taiwan, virtual kidnappers have been known to have a random child screaming in the background to further elevate the parents' level of panic during the phone call. The distraught parents will proceed to pay the "ransom" without thinking to call their child's cell phone. In Mexico, virtual kidnappings have become more prevalent in the past two years, with many of the extortion calls coming from inside prisons. In these cases, jailed gang members threaten to kidnap or kill a family member and demand that payments be made to accomplices on the outside.

Because these criminals rely heavily on obtaining personal information about the intended target, knowing when and where to share that sensitive information is vital to preventing a virtual kidnapping. Knowing the whereabouts of family members throughout the day also is essential. Should a caller claim that a child has been taken when the child should be in class, a quick phone call to the school can defuse the situation before it gets out of hand. Virtual kidnappings are based solely on fear and can be foiled simply by knowing the real whereabouts of a "victim" and keeping one's wits if a ransom call comes in.

Cleaning Out the Victim's Bank Account
May 2, 2006

The bodies of two Austrian backpackers were found in shallow graves in La Paz, Bolivia, on April 3. Bolivian media reported that the victims had been abducted by individuals wearing police uniforms and that their bank cards had been used to withdraw cash from several locations around Bolivia.

It appears the two Austrians were victims of an express kidnapping gone wrong. Under normal circumstances, victims of such kidnappings are robbed of their possessions and then forced to empty their accounts from ATMs. In most cases, the victim is held only while the bank account is emptied, though some express kidnappings can last up to several days while the perpetrators clean out large accounts or wait to collect a quick ransom. Like all confrontational crimes, however, express kidnappings can end in the victim's death.

Express kidnappings are increasingly common in the Third World, particularly in Latin America — and especially in Mexico. Although these kinds of kidnappings commonly start near an outdoor ATM, they can be initiated just as easily during the course of a carjacking, while a traveler is in a taxi operated by a rogue driver or even in a more rural area. Many times the victim has consumed a large amount of alcohol and his inebriation has made him an easy mark.

Because of individual withdrawal limits and other security features regarding the use of debit cards, the perpetrators must hit several ATMs — sometimes as many as five or six in an hour. These multiple withdrawals over a short time, however, can trigger security lockouts of the card, causing the perpetrators to keep their victim for days if the transaction receipt shows a large balance. Some gangs reportedly have kept their victims confined in the trunk of a car for several days while they drain their bank accounts via debit cards. Express kidnappings also can turn into longer-

KIDNAPPING

term kidnap-for-ransom abductions if the criminals discover the victim has significant financial assets — usually by the more-exclusive credit cards in his or her wallet or a business card that identifies the person as a top executive of a well-known company.

Express kidnappings are preferred by small-time criminals for several reasons. Unlike long-term kidnap-for-ransom schemes, the perpetrators generally do not need extensive infrastructure such as safe houses and round-the-clock guards, nor do they need to worry about providing meals and restroom facilities. Express kidnappings also offer the perpetrators a rapid return for their efforts, since the debit account can be cleaned out in a few hours or a ransom quickly paid. Also, holding a victim for such a short time reduces the chances for law enforcement to track down and apprehend the perpetrators.

Because express kidnappings often are carried out by inexperienced kidnappers, the victims are at risk of suffering physical harm or being killed almost immediately, especially if something unexpected happens during the abduction that causes the kidnappers to panic. Another danger, although quite rare, is that the kidnappers will kill the victim even after the accounts are emptied or the ransom paid rather than risk being identified later. Female victims also run the risk of being sexually assaulted by their abductors.

To avoid becoming the victim of an express kidnapping, certain precautions should be taken when traveling. Because taxi drivers often are used by express kidnapping gangs to obtain victims, taxis not affiliated with a reputable company or hotel should be avoided. Travelers also should use ATMs in secure locations such as shopping

99

malls, stores and bank or hotel lobbies rather than on the street, where express kidnappings often are initiated. Travelers also should be aware of indications of a carjacking and practice appropriate preventative or defensive measures. Overall, practicing good situational awareness and surveillance awareness is the best way to avoid becoming a victim.

To minimize loss during an express kidnapping, travelers should consider carrying only cash or, if they must carry a debit card, use one that accesses an account with limited funds, rather than one linked to both checking and savings accounts. The theory here is that the sooner the money runs out, the sooner the victim will be released.

It also is important for victims of any type of kidnapping to try to humanize themselves to their abductors. If possible, some attempt should be made to relate to the kidnappers on a human level — showing pictures of loved ones or talking about sports, for example. If the kidnappers see their victim as a human being rather than an object, the less likely the victim will be killed or abandoned.

The victim also must be prepared to hand over valuables at once. Hesitation or refusal to relinquish valuables could cause an already nervous express kidnapper to resort to violence or, in the case of a simple robbery, cause the perpetrator to abduct the victim with the intention of taking the valuables elsewhere.

During any kidnapping, the most dangerous time for the victim is during the initial abduction — when events are unfolding rapidly, weapons are being brandished and tensions are running high. This period, however, also offers the best chance for escape. In debriefings of hostages, most have said they perceived that a threat was developing, but they did not want to believe it was happening to them. In these early minutes of the kidnapping, however, the perpetrators can lose control of the situation, giving the victim a chance to escape. Of course, if they lose control, the kidnappers could panic and kill the victim on the spot.

Once the initial abduction is over and the kidnappers have control of the victim, the immediate escape window is closed. Now, the victim should cooperate with the kidnappers while continuing to look for viable opportunities to escape. At this point, however, the victim could be making a life-or-death decision: Trying to escape can get one killed — but so can staying put.

High Value Targets: Going for the Big Money
May 3, 2006

In 2003, four gunmen kidnapped U.S. billionaire Eddie Lampert as he left his Connecticut home and held him bound and blindfolded in a bathtub in a cheap motel outside of New Haven. After two days, Lampert succeeded in convincing the increasingly jittery kidnappers to let him go. A short time later, the men ordered a pizza using Lampert's credit card, leading police right to them.

This case is noteworthy because it demonstrates that even bumbling criminals can abduct a high-value target (HVT) in the United States if proper security precautions are not taken. It also demonstrates the importance of the victim's role in securing his or her own freedom.

101

HVT kidnappings, those in which a person of significant personal wealth or status is kidnapped for ransom, are complex — and risky — crimes. These kidnappings are often led by professional criminals and carried out by crews chosen for their specialized skills, such as drivers, gunmen and physical-control specialists. Such kidnappings are also characterized by much more thorough planning than goes into most crimes. In addition to the extensive research of the target, preoperational surveillance and escape plans that might be performed by bank robbers, for example, kidnappers must make arrangements for holding the victim for a prolonged time, making ransom demands and successfully collecting payment.

Because of the complexity of HVT kidnappings — and the high stakes involved — the perpetrators will conduct research on the Internet and use other means to determine the target's assets, behavioral patterns, security measures and vulnerabilities. Plotters might also attempt to enlist the help of someone close to the target, such as household staff, especially workers with access to restricted areas or with knowledge of the target's security. Enlisting the help of insiders is important to kidnappers because insiders can provide valuable information about the target, or even give the kidnappers direct access. Moreover, long-term surveillance of the target will enable the kidnappers to determine when and where he or she is most vulnerable — that is, when the kidnapper has the best chance of carrying out a successful abduction.

During the abduction, kidnappers will display an overwhelming show of force to minimize possible resistance. Once the victim is in their control, the kidnappers will take the victim to a safe house, a location out of plain sight where they can control and operate in with relative freedom. In a prolonged kidnapping, the safe house must be stocked with provisions to hold and feed the victim and staffed with personnel who can provide around-the-clock security for the facility and guard the victim.

In addition to the safe house, kidnappers must make elaborate arrangements for communicating among themselves and with the victim's representatives. These communications are used to negotiate the ransom and arrange for the ransom's delivery and release of the victim. Planning for the ransom-victim exchange requires the abductors to make elaborate arrangements to ensure their security and maximize their chances of escape. These arrangements may include surveillance of the area to check for law enforcement and ensure that the victim's representatives are complying with instructions. In most cases, the kidnappers must also determine a rendezvous point where they will meet after the operation. In the United States, things often go wrong during this delicate exchange, resulting in either the capture of abductors or the abandonment or death of the victim.

Professional criminals prefer HVT kidnappings to the kinds of express and virtual kidnappings carried out by less proficient criminals for several reasons, but primarily because of the potential for a large payoff. They also like the challenge of pulling off a dangerous HVT kidnapping. For career criminals, this challenge is akin to climbing Mount Everest or robbing Fort Knox. Also, unlike armored car heists or bank robberies, kidnappings in the Third World are very rarely reported to the authorities. However, HVT

103

abductions often involve targets with more resources, which allow victims to enlist professional help in tracking the kidnappers. When law enforcement gets involved in HVT cases, police forces in many countries will also devote more resources to capturing the kidnappers.

In the United States, the FBI handles kidnapping cases and has highly sophisticated resources to devote to the problem. Because of this, the overwhelming majority of kidnappers who ask for ransoms — between 95 percent and 98 percent — are caught and convicted. Therefore, kidnapping for ransom is rare in the United States, and HVT kidnappings are even rarer. Most kidnappings for ransom in the United States occur within immigrant communities and are perpetrated by other members of the immigrant group (e.g., Chinese Triad gang members kidnapping the children or spouses of Chinese businesspeople).

The real risk for most U.S. HVTs is overseas, especially in countries like Mexico, Colombia and Iraq, where kidnapping is a well-developed cottage industry. In these places, the industry thrives due to the lack of law and order and the presence of corrupt, often complicit, police.

As in any kidnapping situation, danger to the HVT victim is high — and the victim's ability to respond appropriately is vital. In a well-planned kidnapping, as most HVT abductions are, the rapid execution and seemingly overwhelming force displayed by abductors will leave the victim believing there is little or no choice but to comply. During the initial abduction, resisting the kidnapper sometimes works, but fighting back is probably not worth the risk unless there is a clear way to escape. If the victim notices the threat as it develops — and acts immediately —

he or she stands a better chance of escaping. Conversely, if the victim is caught totally off guard, the kidnappers have all the advantages.

Potential victims can take precautionary measures to avoid an HVT kidnapping. The most effective and obvious measure is to employ a personal security detail. HVTs with security details are seldom kidnapped, and security details that add route analysis, protective surveillance and variance of routes and schedules to their repertoires seldom lose their charges. Security details and HVTs should maintain a high level of situational awareness about their surroundings, especially near home and work and at any regular appointments or announced public events. On the route itself, attention must be paid to choke points and other stops that would make ideal locations for attack. By being aware of anything unusual or out of place, the security detail and the HVT have a good chance of spotting hostile surveillance or preparations for abduction.

In addition to maintaining physical security, other precautions can be taken to make an HVT a more difficult target for kidnappers. The first is privacy protection. By minimizing the amount of personal information available to the public, such as information on the Internet and in newspapers, HVTs can frustrate the planning efforts of potential kidnappers. To this end, household staff and employees should be briefed on the need to protect privacy and educated as to what kind of questions constitute attempts to gather sensitive information.

Household staff, as well as contractors and temporary employees, should also be thoroughly vetted. Security directors and HVTs should learn about the personal lives of staff members and be aware of new people in their lives. These measures can mitigate a kidnapper's ability to infiltrate the household.

Keeping the HVT's car in a secured parking place, concealed if possible, prevents kidnappers from tampering with it or determining whether the HVT is visiting a particular location. HVTs and their drivers should also consider being trained in escape-and-evasion driving. All of these measures should be practiced aggressively in countries where kidnapping is rampant.

HVTs who fall victim to kidnappings have some options to mitigate the risk of death. One useful approach is to humanize themselves to their captors. By appearing more like a person and less like an object, the victim could reduce his or her chances of being killed, or cause the captors to hesitate at the crucial moment. To accomplish this, the victim should establish a rapport with the kidnappers, being careful to avoid undermining captors' efforts to preserve their anonymity.

Victims should try to maintain physical health and vigor by eating, drinking and exercising whenever possible. It is also important to keep the mind sharp by reading books or performing other kinds of mental exercises. In the event of a rescue or escape attempt, events could unfold very quickly and the victim needs to be lucid enough to react accordingly. Once the escape window has closed, the victim should cooperate with the kidnappers but continue to look for every viable opportunity to escape. During a rescue attempt, the victim should be prepared to assume a position that eliminates the chances of being mistaken for a kidnapper or caught in the crossfire between rescuers and kidnappers.

High-profile individuals, especially those traveling to high-risk countries, should plan for the worst. HVTs should obtain kidnap and ransom (K&R) insurance, including negotiation services if they are offered. The professional negotiator — as opposed to family members or friends — will know how far to push the kidnappers without risking the victim's well-being. However, HVTs should never disclose the fact that they have K&R insurance to anyone. If potential kidnappers know an individual is covered, that person becomes a more attractive target because of the almost-guaranteed payoff.

It is important for the negotiating team to have a clear plan and speak with a single voice. If there is the slightest chance that disputes will arise over how best to deal with the situation, this should be discussed ahead of time. One person should be appointed to make decisions and speak for the family. This is especially important in the period before the ransom delivery and hostage release, when events begin to break rapidly. Additionally, these discussions should include a decision on whether to call the authorities in the event of kidnapping, especially in a foreign country.

Because of corruption and ineptitude among police and security forces in many countries, reporting a kidnapping could get the victim killed. The risks here are that corrupt police officials could be cooperating with kidnappers, or ill-equipped security forces could bungle a rescue attempt. Under such circumstances, it is best for the victim's family or employer to call the insurance company first — and perhaps consider not involving the local authorities at all.

When the Message or Money is the Motive
May 4, 2006

U.S. journalist Jill Carroll survived nearly three months in captivity following her Jan. 7 abduction in Baghdad, Iraq. Although those holding her made certain political demands, it is possible she was freed following a ransom payment and not because the U.S. government agreed to any concessions. Carroll's abduction is an example of the role played by kidnappers in modern urban warfare — for motives of politics or greed.

In political kidnappings, a person or people are abducted by a group for the purpose of changing a government's behavior — or at least getting that government's attention. Kidnapping or hostage-taking, especially of high-value targets, is a tactic preferred by political groups because it allows the group to gain media attention and compels a government to enter into dialogue. The kidnappers know, however, that the targeted government probably will not meet their demands, and so they hold the victim as a form of pressure. This is why the victims of such kidnappings generally are held for a much longer period than those abducted for ransom. In the kidnappers' thinking, the longer that pressure lasts, the more their message is heard and the more leverage they have.

The 1979-1981 Iranian hostage crisis, in which militant students overran the U.S. Embassy in Tehran and held 52 embassy personnel hostage for more than a year, is an example of a politically motivated kidnapping. The students demanded the return of the exiled Shah and the release of Iranian assets frozen in the United States.

Although some kidnappings appear to be politically motivated, they are in fact carried out for the money. A kidnapping gang that tries to disguise itself as a political group and political groups that kidnap in order to finance their operations are such examples. The guerrilla group Revolutionary Armed Forces of Colombia, for example, turned to kidnapping to finance its operations after one of its sources of funding ran out with the fall of the Soviet Union.

In war zones or in areas where anti-government insurgencies are taking place, we see both kinds of kidnappings: those motivated by politics and those motivated by greed. And sometimes the two overlap. During Lebanon's civil war in the 1980s, various militias and criminal gangs abducted several U.S. citizens and then sold them to another group with a political agenda. This Beirut business model is being seen in Iraq today. In these chaotic conditions, kidnappers can take advantage of the lack of law and order, easy access to weapons and territory that could be denied to government forces.

In war zones or areas controlled by insurgents, it becomes easier to hold victims for long periods because they are held in an area denied to government forces or controlled by a group sympathetic to the kidnappers. This enables the kidnappers to utilize a more-extensive infrastructure of safe houses, lookouts and guards. It also makes a rescue operation extremely difficult — usually beyond the capabilities of local police and requiring military Special Forces units.

The best way to prevent falling victim to a political or war-zone kidnapping is to avoid high-risk situations. Journalists, Western aid workers and employees of other nongovernmental organizations often fail to realize they are

109

just as viable a target as a government or military official. These professionals often believe their noncombatant or observer status will protect them from such kidnappings, though militants and criminal gangs, especially those focused on the profit aspect of a kidnapping, may not share that sentiment. In fact, because these people rarely employ personal protective details, they are easy targets and extremely vulnerable to abduction.

One of the most effective methods of preventing politically motivated kidnappings or kidnappings in war zones is to employ bodyguards. Every Westerner, especially one of considerable wealth or status, should take this precaution while traveling in a war zone such as Iraq or a high-risk area such as Latin America. Bodyguards should be familiar with the local area and adequately trained to deal with ambush situations. In many cases, private protective security firms are hired for this purpose.

Although one of the most dangerous times for any kidnapping victim is during the initial snatch, this is especially true in a war zone, where weapons are ubiquitous and inhabitants might have become desensitized to taking human life. Just as in other kidnappings, however, the only real escape window could open during this time. Many of the same techniques used to increase chances of survival in other types of kidnappings also apply to those motivated by politics, remembering that the escape window will be open only for a brief time, especially for victims held deep in hostile territory. Beyond the basic rules for humanizing oneself with the captors, every kidnapping victim should work in small ways to establish limits and maintain dignity. Victims can indicate, for example, that they will be more cooperative if they are allowed small concessions such as bathing and changing clothes regularly and not being forced to eat off of the floor.

In the absence of law and order, or complete government control in high-risk areas, kidnapping for political or financial reasons has become common. Those who travel or work in these areas should take precautions to prevent becoming the victim of a kidnapping — and be prepared should they be abducted.

When the Battle over Children Turns Desperate
May 5, 2006

A preliminary hearing has been set for May 31 in the case of Mary Jane Byrd, a mother who allegedly abducted her 4-year-old daughter from Washington, D.C., 13 years ago in defiance of a court order giving the child's father visitation rights. Byrd was arrested in April on a felony charge of kidnapping by a parent in one of the nation's longest-running missing-child cases. Although the phenomenon of familial kidnappings is not new, attention to the subject in recent years has led to tougher laws to deal with it.

Most familial kidnappings are carried out to contravene a court-ordered custody arrangement, especially when one parent believes he or she has been deprived of rightful custody. In many cases, however, a child is abducted by one parent or other family member because of a perceived dangerous situation, such as sexual or physical abuse of the child, or unsafe behavior exhibited by the custodial parent, such as drug abuse or other criminal activity. The custody dispute is often between the child's biological parents, although other family members, such as grandparents, aunts and uncles, sometimes are involved.

Children also are abducted by a parent or other family member as a means of controlling or psychologically harming the custodial parent, or as revenge for real or perceived wrongs by one family member against another. In other cases, certain types of mental illnesses suffered by the noncustodial family member, such as paranoid delusions or severe sociopathy, may lead that individual to commit the abduction. This risk can be exacerbated if the noncustodial family member feels court judgments regarding custody are unfair.

The latest statistics from the National Center for Missing and Exploited Children (NCMEC) show that out of almost 798,000 children reported missing in 2002, more than 200,000 — about one quarter — were believed to have been abducted by family members. Unlike other forms of kidnapping, familial abductions are not carried out for monetary gain, to make a political statement or to gain media attention. In most cases, in fact, the kidnapper aims to completely drop off the radar with the child, perhaps with the help of a religious or community group that supports the move. A strengthening of the law in Washington, D.C., changing parental abductions from a misdemeanor to a potential felony, is one example of efforts to solve these kidnapping cases.

One of the best ways to prevent a familial kidnapping is by ensuring that communications between parents, and between parents and children, are healthy and open. Not only can open communications reduce friction, it also can help the children better understand the rules of custody, perhaps making them less willing to go along on an unplanned trip with an unauthorized family member. Parents involved in a joint-custody situation should work together to establish clear, mutually understood and agreed-upon arrangements. These should follow legally binding custody guidelines, but also leave room for legal review should conditions change. Parents are more likely to abduct when they feel they have no legal recourse.

Because of consistent cases of familial abductions from schools, most have enacted measures to guard against these incidents. Custodial parents, therefore, should work with school officials to ensure clear understanding of parental rules about such things as early or unscheduled pickups and identification of individuals authorized to pick up the child.

According to a governmental study cited by the NCMEC, there are risk indicators that can provide some advance warning of a plot to kidnap a minor family member. The greatest risk that such a kidnapping will occur is within the first four or five years after a divorce or separation of households, or when there has been a previous threat or actual abduction. Another indicator is the perception by the noncustodial spouse or family member that the child is being abused or mistreated by the custodial family member. Custodial parents also should be alert to the threat at times when relations are especially strained between them and noncustodial family members.

If a parent who is a citizen of another country loses custody in a U.S. court, he or she might abduct the children and take them back to their home country. Once there, the legal, political and cultural considerations that come into play can make getting the child back extremely complicated, if not impossible.

Parents can take precautions to increase the chances of a favorable resolution to a familial kidnapping. The most effective of these include having good-quality, up-to-date (every six months for children age 6 and under) photos of the children available, as well as photographs of potential abductors. Parents also should know the description and license plate numbers of the other parent's or family members' vehicles. In addition, custodial parents should try not to allow alienation from the other parent to become so severe that they know little or nothing about the other's living arrangements, support systems or circumstances. In many cases, feared abductions turn out to be nothing more than scheduling misunderstandings. However, after taking reasonable steps to resolve the situation on his or her own, the custodial parent should contact police early and report the abduction.

Children, even small ones, also can be educated in this regard. At the very least, they should be asked to memorize their home phone number, including area code, and taught how to use the phone. It also is a good idea, under any circumstances, to have the child's fingerprints on file, even if done with a home fingerprinting kit.

Sexual-Exploitation: The Risk of Death is High
May 8, 2006

Jackie Barron Wilson was executed in Huntsville, Texas, on May 4 for the 1988 abduction, rape and murder of a 5-year-old girl. Although he proclaimed his innocence until the end, Wilson was convicted of taking Maggie Rhodes from her bedroom in Arlington, Texas, and in the space of a few hours sexually assaulting and killing her. The case illustrates many of the characteristics of sexual-exploitation kidnappings, including the high mortality rate for victims.

According to the U.S. Justice Department's National Incidence Studies of Missing, Abducted, Runaway and Throwaway Children (NISMART), 797,500 children were reported missing in 1999. Of that figure, 203,900 were believed to have been victims of family abductions and 58,200 abducted by nonfamily members. The report also said 115 children were the victims of the most serious, long-term nonfamily abductions called "stereotypical kidnappings." In these cases, the child is transported a distance of 50 miles or more, and then either killed, held for ransom or held with the abductor's intent of keeping the child permanently. In nearly half of these cases, the child was exploited sexually, and in at least 40 percent of these cases, the child was killed.

In a sexual-exploitation kidnapping of a child, sexual assault often is the sole motivation. When ransom demands are made — which is rare — they usually are an afterthought, often made after the victim has been killed. In about half of the cases, the victim's body is concealed rather than left for authorities to find. Therefore, many of the victims of this crime are never found.

According to the Washington State Office of the Attorney General, the majority of sexual-exploitation kidnappings are carried out by males against females. The kidnapper in these cases averages 27 years of age, usually lives alone or with his parents, and holds a low-wage job. Furthermore, two-thirds of those arrested for sexual exploitation kidnapping have been arrested for crimes against children before — mostly of a sexual nature. The offenders in these cases often repeat their previous methods in these crimes, making it easy for law enforcement to determine a pattern and identify the perpetrator, although this can be done only after multiple offenses are committed.

Most of the perpetrators live near their victims or have a legitimate reason for being in proximity to the victim, such as day laborers or other contracted labor. This happened in the case of 14-year-old Elizabeth Smart, who allegedly was abducted from her bedroom in Utah by Brian Mitchell, who had been employed at her home to do roofing work.

In sexual-exploitation kidnappings, unlike for-ransom or political kidnappings, the abductor often has no interest in keeping the victim alive or eventually releasing the victim unharmed. On the contrary, the repetitive nature of the crime means the abductor is more likely to kill the victim in order to cover his tracks, and thus ensure that he can continue his behavior. Most victims in these cases, in fact, are killed within the first three hours of the abduction.

Because most kidnappings of this nature occur close to the home and school, parents and children may feel a false sense of security. The best deterrents to this kind of crime, therefore, are close supervision of the children or knowledge of their whereabouts, situational awareness and aggressive

116

reporting of suspicious people. In addition, community situational awareness adds another layer of security. Neighbors and even service personnel such as mail carriers, utility workers and delivery drivers should be aware of unusual behavior in the area and be encouraged to report it.

Starting at an early age, children should be made aware of the threat and taught how to respond to it. Initiatives like the national "Stranger Danger" program, which has been run by local police departments for decades, focus on children from kindergarten to fifth grade. Parents should supplement these programs by discussing the threat frankly and openly with their children.

Children should be taught never to approach an unknown car or individual, and to run from any stranger who approaches. Most children will exhibit submissive behavior when confronted by a threatening situation, which often allows a kidnapper the opportunity, however brief, to strike. In the case of abduction, hesitation can lead to tragedy — as shown in the surveillance tape of the 2004 abduction of 11-year-old Carlie Brucia in Sarasota, Fla.

Parents also should employ an attitude of suspicion when it comes to strangers. Extreme caution should be exercised by parents when allowing unknown individuals access to the home. In the Smart case, the victim's father hired an unemployed drifter to do roofing work on the house, placing him in close proximity to his daughter.

In the case of any child abduction, the first hours after the crime are critical. Most missing-child reports are made an hour after the child is first noticed missing — and the child may have been abducted long before that. Given the critical three-hour window, this is often far too late. Parents should have up-to-date photographs and fingerprints of their child readily available, and be able to describe what the child was wearing and the places he or she went that day.

Although sexual-exploitation kidnappings are rare, the child victims are more likely to be killed than those kidnapped for ransom or in custody disputes. Parents should take steps to minimize their children's vulnerability to this crime — and act aggressively in reporting the disappearance of a child.

The Proactive Tool of Protective Intelligence
Nov. 7, 2007

On Nov. 4, 46-year-old Spanish businessman Edelmiro Manuel Pérez Merelles was freed from captivity after being held for nearly two weeks by kidnappers who grabbed him from his vehicle in the Mexico City metropolitan area. The fact that a kidnapping occurred in Mexico is not at all unusual. What is unusual is the enormous press coverage the case received, largely because of the audacity and brutality of the attackers.

Pérez Merelles was snatched from his car Oct. 22 after a gang of heavily armed assailants blocked his vehicle and, in full view of witnesses, killed his bodyguard/driver, delivering a coup de grâce shot to the back of his head. The abductors then shoved the driver's body into the trunk of Pérez Merelles' car, which was later found abandoned. After the abduction, when the family balked at the exorbitant amount of ransom demanded, the kidnappers reportedly upped the ante by sending two of Pérez Merelles' fingers to his family. A ransom finally was paid and Pérez Merelles was released in good health, though sans the fingers.

In a world in which militants and criminals appear increasingly sophisticated and brutal, this case highlights the need for protective intelligence (PI) to augment traditional security measures.

Action vs. Reaction

As any football player knows, action is always faster than reaction. That principle provides offensive players with a slight edge over their opponents on the defense, because the offensive players know the snap count that will signal the beginning of the play. Now, some crafty defensive players will anticipate or jump the snap to get an advantage over the offensive players, but that anticipation is an action in itself and not a true reaction. This same principle of action and reaction is applicable to security operations. For example, when members of an abduction team launch an assault against a target's vehicle, they have the advantage of tactical surprise over the target and any security personnel protecting the target. This advantage can be magnified significantly if the target lacks the proper mindset and freezes in response to the attack.

Even highly trained security officers who have been schooled in attack recognition and in responding under pressure to attacks against their principal are at a disadvantage once an attack is launched. This is because, in addition to having the element of tactical surprise, the assailants also have conducted surveillance and have planned their attack. Therefore, they presumably have come prepared — with the number of assailants and the right weaponry — to overcome any security assets in place. Simply put, the criminals will not attack unless they believe they have the advantage. Not all attacks succeed, of course. Sometimes the attackers will botch the attempt, and sometimes security personnel are good enough — or lucky enough — to regain the initiative and fight off the attack or otherwise escape. In general, however, once an attack is launched, the attackers have the advantage over the defender, who not only is reacting but also is simultaneously trying to identify the source, location and direction of the attack and assess the number of assailants and their armament.

Furthermore, if a gang is brazen enough to conduct a serious crime such as a kidnapping for ransom, which carries stiff penalties in most countries, chances are the same group is capable of committing homicide during the crime. So, using the kidnapping example, the gang will account for the presence of any security officers in its planning and will devise a way to neutralize those officers — as the attackers neutralized the bodyguard in the Pérez Merelles abduction.

Even if the target is traveling in an armored vehicle, the attackers will plan a way to immobilize it, breach the armor and get to their victim. In a kidnapping scenario, once the target's vehicle is stopped or disabled, the assailants can place an explosive device on top of it, forcing the occupants to open the door or risk death — a tactic witnessed several times in Latin America — or they can use hand tools to pry it open like a can of sardines if given enough time. Since most armored vehicles use the car's factory-installed door-lock system, techniques used by car thieves, such as using master keys or punching out the locks, also can be used effectively against an immobilized armored vehicle.

This same principle applies to physical security measures at buildings. Measures such as badge readers, closed-circuit TV coverage, metal detectors, cipher locks and so forth are an important part of any security plan — though they have finite utility. In many cases assailants have mapped out, quantified and then defeated or bypassed physical security devices. Physical security devices require human interaction and a proactive security program to optimize their effectiveness.

Armed guards, armored vehicles and physical security devices can all be valuable tools, but they can be defeated by attackers who have planned an attack and then put it into play at the time and place of their choosing. Clearly, a way is needed to deny attackers the advantage of striking when and where they choose or, even better, to stop an attack before it can be launched. In other words, security officers must play on the action side of the action/reaction equation. That is where PI comes in.

Protective Intelligence

In simple terms, PI is the process used to identify and assess threats. A well-designed PI program will have a number of distinct and crucial components or functions, but the most important of these are countersurveillance, investigations and analysis. The first function, countersurveillance, serves as the eyes and ears of the PI team. As noted above, kidnapping gangs conduct extensive preoperational surveillance. But all criminals — stalkers, thieves, lone wolves, militant groups, etc. — engage in some degree of preoperational surveillance, though the length of this surveillance will vary depending on the actor and the circumstances. A purse-snatcher might case a potential target for a few seconds, while a kidnapping gang might conduct surveillance of a potential target for weeks. The degree of surveillance tradecraft — from very clumsy to highly sophisticated — also will widely vary, depending on the operatives' training and street skills.

It is while conducting this surveillance that someone with hostile intentions is most apt to be detected, making this the point in the attack cycle that potential violence can most easily be disrupted or prevented. This is what makes countersurveillance such a valuable proactive tool.

Although countersurveillance teams are valuable, they cannot operate in a vacuum. They need to be part of a larger PI program that includes the analytical and investigative functions. Investigation and analysis are two closely related yet distinct components that can help focus the countersurveillance operations on the most likely or most vulnerable targets, analyze the observations of the countersurveillance team and investigate any suspicious individuals observed.

Without an analytical function, it is difficult for countersurveillance operatives to note when the same person or vehicle has been encountered on different shifts or at different sites. In fact, countersurveillance operations are far less valuable when they are conducted without databasing or analyzing what the countersurveillance teams observe over time and distance.

Investigations also are important. Most often, something that appears unusual to a countersurveillance operative has a logical and harmless explanation, though it is difficult to make that determination without an investigative unit to follow-up on red flags.

The investigative and analytical functions also are crucial in assessing communications from mentally disturbed individuals, for tracking the activities of activist or extremist groups and for attempting to identify and assess individuals who make anonymous threats via telephone or mail. Mentally disturbed individuals have long posed a substantial (and still underestimated) threat to both prominent people and average citizens in the United States. In fact, mentally disturbed individuals have killed far more prominent people (including President James Garfield, Bobby Kennedy and John Lennon) than militants have in terrorist attacks.

Furthermore, nearly all of those who have committed attacks have self-identified or otherwise come to the attention of authorities before the attack was carried out. Because of this, PI teams ensure that no mentally disturbed person is summarily dismissed as a "harmless nut" until he or she has been thoroughly investigated and his or her communications carefully analyzed and databased. Databasing is crucial because it allows the tenor of correspondence from a mentally disturbed individual to be monitored over time and compared with earlier missives in order to identify signs of a deteriorating mental state or a developing intent to commit violence. PI teams will often consult mental health professionals in such cases to assist with psycholinguistic and psychological evaluations.

Not all threats from the mentally disturbed come from outside a company or organization, however. Although the common perception following a workplace incident is that the employee "just snapped," in most cases the factors leading to the violent outburst have been building up for a long time and the assailant has made detailed plans. Because of this, workplace or school shootings seldom occur randomly. In most cases, the perpetrator has targeted a specific individual or set of individuals who the shooter believes is responsible for his plight. Therefore, PI teams also will work closely with human-resources managers and employee mental health programs to try to identify early on those employees who have the potential to commit acts of workplace violence.

In workplace settings as well as other potential threat areas, PI operatives also can aid other security officers by providing them with photographs and descriptions of any person identified as a potential threat. The person identified as the potential target also can be briefed and the information shared with that person's administrative assistants, family members and household staff.

Another crucial function of a PI team is to "red team," or to look at the security program from the outside and help identify vulnerabilities. Most security looks from the inside out, but PI provides the ability to look from the outside in. In the executive protection realm, this can include an analysis of the principal's schedule and transportation routes in order to determine the most vulnerable times and places. Countersurveillance or even overt security assets can then be focused on these crucial locations.

Red teams also sometimes perform cyberstalker research. That is, they study a potential target through a criminal or mentally disturbed person's eyes — attempting to obtain as much open-source and public-record information

KIDNAPPING

on that target as possible in order to begin a surveillance operation. Such a project helps determine what sensitive information is available regarding a particular target and highlights how that information could be used by a criminal planning an attack.

Red teams also will attempt to invade a facility in order to test access control or to conduct surveillance on the operations in an effort to identify vantage points (or "perches") that would most likely be used by someone surveilling the facility. Once the perches around one's facility are identified, activities at those sites can be monitored, making it more difficult for assailants to conduct preoperational surveillance at will.

One other advantage to PI operations is that, being amorphous by nature, they are far more difficult for a potential assailant to detect than are traditional security measures. Even if one PI operative is detected — regardless of whether the team has identified its targets — the surveillers' anxiety will increase because they likely will not know whether the person they encounter is a countersurveillance operative.

This combination of countersurveillance, analysis and investigation can be applied in a number of other creative and proactive ways to help keep potential threats off balance and deny them the opportunity to take the initiative. Although a large global corporation or government might require a large PI team, these core functions can be performed by a skilled, compact team, or even by one person. For example, a person living in a high-threat environment such as Mexico City can acquire the skills to perform his or her own analysis of route and schedule, and can run surveillance detection routes in order to smoke out hostile operations.

The details of the Pérez Merelles kidnapping indicate that it was a professionally planned and well-executed operation. Crimes of this caliber do not occur on the spur of the moment. They require extensive surveillance, intelligence gathering and planning — the very types of activities that are vulnerable to detection through the proactive tool of PI.

CHAPTER 5: Asymmetrical Combat

Dealing With an Armed and Unexpected Assailant
April 23, 2007

As they go about their day, most people in the civilized world give very little thought to the possibility of having to fend off an attacker. When law-abiding citizens who practice good situational awareness are attacked, those attacks will take them by surprise. Even if they are armed, their weapon will most likely be holstered or otherwise unavailable for the critical first seconds of the attack. Hence, all people — armed and unarmed — should consider seeking training in the principles of empty-hand self-defense. Obviously, not having a weapon handy is a distinct disadvantage in modern-day criminal confrontations because most violent criminals use weapons — guns, blades and clubs. Criminal attackers also come in multiples as often as not, although it may not in all cases be necessary for a person who has the right goals in mind — escape and survival — to deal physically with more than one attacker at a time.

In our view, it is not possible to teach self-defense from the printed page, or even with video. Nothing comes even close to in-person, physical training from expert teachers who try their best to provide the student with safe but realistic training scenarios. This report should be taken as guidance, not training — guidance that can be incorporated into the reader's formal self-defense training.

To advise people on decisions that could affect their survival carries with it grave responsibilities. This is one reason why many martial arts and self-defense teachers and writers shy away from discussing defense against armed assailants, especially those armed with guns. It is one thing to make an error in judgment that can land one in the hospital with a broken bone or two; it is quite another when the same error might get you or a loved one killed. The usual way out is simply to advise compliance with an armed assailant, but, as we shall see, while simulated compliance as a temporary strategy can be useful, total compliance can sometimes be more dangerous than resistance.

The facts won't alter themselves simply because we'd rather not face them. In a confrontation with an armed or with multiple assailants, we are already in a potentially life-threatening situation. Any course we take, including doing nothing at all, can be fatal if things go the wrong way. Thus, there are no guarantees in such situations, only better or worse courses of action.

Handguns: Machines with Limitations

By far the most common firearms used in violent criminal confrontations are handguns, i.e., semiautomatic pistols and double-action revolvers. STRATFOR recommends that students of self-defense seek training in the use of firearms, even if they don't contemplate carrying one. One reason for this recommendation is that it is useful to have a general understanding of how guns work, what they can and cannot do, and to get some feel for the skill level needed to use one effectively. And if one is fortunate enough to find self-defense instructors who can teach reliable methods for disarming a gun-wielding attacker, it would be wise to understand how the gun — now in your hands — operates.

Guns kill thousands of people every year. They are deadly and must be treated with respect. However, a few facts may help put this into realistic perspective. Guns are machines and, like all machines, they have their limitations. With modern guns, the greatest limitation of all is the operator. Shooting a handgun accurately, even under the controlled conditions of a firing range, is a perishable skill that requires initial training and a great deal of subsequent practice.

It is a mathematical fact that an error of a millimeter in aiming a handgun is multiplied geometrically, the farther the target is from the muzzle of the gun. Because guns are held in fallible human hands, there is always a certain degree of error. For the self-defense student, the important lesson in this is that distance means safety, and the more distance the better.

Range (simply expressed as how far the bullet will travel) is not the important factor. Projectiles fired from a handgun can travel much farther than the distances within which they can be fired accurately, even when fired by experts. Depending on the environmental conditions and the skills of the shooter, it might be said that at 50 yards or more, anyone who is hit by a bullet fired from a handgun is a victim of bad luck. The world record for the 50-yard dash is around five seconds. When an unskilled shooter is under stress, in poor environmental conditions and shooting at a moving target, that relatively safe distance becomes much, much less. Indeed, even at very short distances, misses are common. *Distance enhances safety.*

Equally, because accurate shooting at a distance depends on aligning the weapon's sights correctly on the target, shooting a handgun at a moving target is in itself a special skill, not easily acquired, and certainly not commonly found. *Motion enhances safety.*

Anything the target does that forces the shooter to realign his shooting stance and re-acquire his target in the gun's sight picture affects his accuracy. This can be accomplished by moving at an angle to the imaginary line that emanates from the gun. Think of it as a laser beam. (People are sometimes taught to run from a shooter in a zig-zag pattern. This may not be the best choice, if the pattern repeatedly brings one across the imaginary laser beam emanating from the gun.) *Changing the angle enhances safety.*

Accurate shooting depends on good visibility of the target. A shooter who cannot see his target is just guessing. Even factors that partially obscure the target, such as dim light, an advertisement-covered store window rendered partially opaque by reflections or a thin screen of shrubbery, affects accuracy. This is technically called concealment, and *even partial concealment enhances safety.*

Handguns are not all-powerful, although some are more powerful than others. The velocity of bullets of a given weight fired from any gun depends mostly on the power of the powder charge that propels it out of the barrel (technically not an explosion, but a contained "burn" generating a rapid expansion of gases). The energy with which a bullet hits its target depends on the bullet's speed and its weight. Because handguns are held in the hands, then, their designed "power" is limited by simple Newtonian physics, i.e., for every action there is an equal and opposite reaction. In the case of guns, this is known as recoil, and too much recoil limits the shooter's ability to control — or even hold onto — the gun and take a second shot. Handguns are by design necessity less "powerful" than other kinds of guns.

What all this means is that bullets fired from a handgun are limited in what they can penetrate, and in the degree of damage they can inflict on the human body. Anything that will stop a bullet is called "cover," and there are a great many objects in the environment that will stop most handgun bullets cold: e.g., a masonry wall, the trunk of a tree, the wheel assembly and engine block of a truck or car. Even partial cover is better than none at all; anything a bullet strikes or penetrates on its way to its intended target is likely to deflect it or possibly fragment it. Even if it is partial, *cover enhances safety.*

Obviously, given a choice between mere concealment and cover, it is best to choose cover; in escaping, however, take whatever comes first and look for opportunities for improvement.

In tactical order, these principles — *motion, distance, angle, concealment and cover* (MDACC) — should be kept in mind when attempting to escape from a shooter.

131

Shoulder and Automatic Weapons

Because they are more difficult to conceal than handguns, shoulder weapons and automatic weapons (the latter defined as guns that keep firing as long as you hold down the trigger or until the magazine is empty) are less often seen in violent criminal confrontations. This is fortunate, because these guns, in general, are more dangerous. Rifles are easier to shoot with accuracy at greater distances than handguns, and most of them are more powerful; shotguns fire a large number of projectiles at one time, thus increasing the chances of being hit. The same is true for automatic weapons, which fire a great many projectiles at the target in a short time.

Nevertheless, the MDACC principles still apply, since under the conditions for their deployment (which we will explore later) there is no other viable option.

Collateral Damage: When You Are Not the Target

Random shots from violent criminal encounters kill a few people every year in this country. In some cases, one hears gunfire nearby but cannot immediately tell what direction it is coming from. Taking a leaf from the combat soldier's book, if this happens and you are caught in the open, drop to the ground without hesitation. This provides you with partial concealment and partial cover. If you are on a sidewalk and traffic permits, consider rolling into the gutter: The masonry curb will improve your cover. Begin looking and listening to determine where the fire is coming from. Once you can answer this question, start looking around for better cover.

132

However, *do not move* until you know where the shots are coming from, unless bullet strikes near you force you to move. When you do move, use the guidance MDACC to make a safe escape.

Blades, Short and Long

People — especially people brought up in developed Western countries — fear blades. This has not always been the case. There are Americans still alive today who will tell you that as little boys in grammar school, they were encouraged, if not required, to carry a pocketknife to sharpen their pencils.

Our very recent ancestors carried and used blades as secondary weapons of war and defense. We use knives every day in our kitchens and push lawn mowers — motorized blades traveling at high speeds — on our lawns. Given this, our almost visceral fear of blades used as weapons is puzzling. In a self-defense scenario, this attitude is also not useful.

Blades are sharp extensions of the arms. As such, their reach at any moment only extends to the length of the attacker's arm, plus the length of the blade. Statistically, we can forget about thrown knives; the number of people living on the earth at any one time who can throw a knife with force and accuracy without first pacing off the distance and practicing would not fill a small auditorium.

Thus, outside a circle of about three feet for knives and five feet at most, perhaps, for longer blades (excepting swords), a blade-wielding attacker is harmless. What professional self-defense instructors should also teach is that in the right circumstances, being *inside* that circle of sharpness — very close to the attacker — can be a momentary safe haven as well. Again, we have no intention of teaching specific self-defense moves here, but would encourage readers to take up this guidance with their professional instructors. Blade attacks also can be defended against — momentarily, to facilitate escape and survival — using items found in a normal environment. A good self-defense course should incorporate training in identifying and using these items. One example is a light chair, which can be easily wielded and can deflect an attacker's blade.

Readers should accept, however, that any violent encounter at close quarters with a blade-wielding attacker is likely to result in injury — perhaps more likely even than an encounter with someone wielding a gun. The good news is that such injuries are often not life-threatening or even incapacitating, as long as the victim keeps his or her head and acts decisively to escape and survive.

The Good Old Louisville Slugger

Clubs — which include sticks, lengths of pipe and baseball bats — are almost exclusively used as striking (versus thrusting) weapons by untrained persons. The physics of these attacks is easy enough to understand. Safety lies completely outside, and momentarily close inside, their circle of effective impact. Think of a bunt, in baseball, versus a full swing of the bat. Self-defense courses should include training in these concepts.

A word of caution about heavy striking weapons: Strikes with them are intended to and often do break bones, and broken bones can quickly render one immediately incapacitated — more so than knife wounds or even most gunshot wounds. Unconsciousness or the inability to use one's legs makes escape impossible.

Analysis of Armed Confrontations

STRATFOR does not believe in creating educational scenarios for their own sake. For every possible set of circumstances, good or bad, there are a great many outcomes, not all of them predictable. Nonetheless, sometimes a notional scenario can focus the inquiry.

Here is one: Let's say you have worked late and, on your way home, remember that you need milk. Your favorite convenience store is on the way and you pull into the parking lot right in front of the door. You are tired, and although your security awareness training will have told you that you should scan such places visually through the windows before entering them late at night, you don't. We are all human. You walk right in. As you enter, the first thing you see is that the store clerks are standing together behind the counter, their eyes wide with fear. A man is standing in front of them with his back to you, and as he hears you come in, he starts to turn his body in your direction. As he turns, you see the pistol in his hands, raised at shoulder level. He is saying something as the muzzle of the pistol comes around to bear on you. You are one step inside the door, holding it open with one hand. The door opens inward. The man is about ten feet away.

What are your options at this moment?

Let's dissect the situation, adding a few notional facts. The store is located on a busy thoroughfare with street lights. Directly across this street is an all-night self-service gas station, brightly lit, with several cars at the pumps. Directly behind the convenience store is a large residential subdivision. The store is a brick building with a plate glass front, partially plastered with posters. The door by which you entered is centered in the plate glass storefront. The front parking area of the store is bathed in light, which is dimmer at the sides and fades to relative darkness toward the back. There is no fencing around the store, only a narrow roadway around the back for deliveries and the front street of the first row of houses in the subdivision.

You also know three more things at that moment: The gun is not yet pointed at you; the man is talking, not shooting; and his solid, two-handed grip on the gun suggests that he may have had some training and is at least physically ready to shoot.

Should you escape at that moment? Given the circumstances, probably yes. Imagine for a moment that the man is already shooting at you, which would of course obviate the need to choose. If you step quickly out the door, there will be partial concealment and partial cover between you and the shooter, before the muzzle of the gun can track you. If you make a sharp right or left and run parallel to the window (versus straight across the street to the well-lit gas station), you present a target moving at right angles to the shooter's stance. The farther you go along that path, the better cover the store's plate glass will present, since bullets fired at it will hit it at increasingly acute angles, degrading their accuracy. Once you reach the end of the plate glass

136

(perhaps three running steps) and turn sharply behind the brick side wall, you have attained complete cover and concealment. You can disappear into the dimly lit housing complex before the shooter can get out the door and follow you. Will he follow you, risking exposure to more witnesses and 911 calls from alarmed residents? Probably not. Using the formula MDACC, you have escaped and survived.

Emergency survival situations often come about as the cascade effect of a series of small errors. So, continuing our scenario to the next step, let's say that instead of escaping as described above, you come all the way inside, the door closing behind you. Your eyes fix hypnotically on the muzzle of the gun, which by now is pointed directly at you. In your shocked state, you struggle to understand what the man is telling you. Part of you knows that understanding and following his orders is critical: If you make him repeat them, he may shoot instead of talk. You are in more trouble at this moment than ever before in your life. You just walked into the zone of combat.

When to Comply and When to Resist

However, the man is talking, not shooting, and this is an important fact. There are two reasons why someone deploys a weapon in a situation such as this: first, to harm or kill. If he is already shooting, MDACC comes immediately into play. The second reason is to intimidate for compliance, which is what is now happening. These dynamics can change from one to the other in an instant, but for the moment the most important thing for us to understand is what the man's intentions are.

He tells you to do exactly as he says, or he will shoot you. In that moment, you should be thinking, "If I *do* comply, he *won't* shoot me." Your course of action at this point is to comply, see what happens next, and look for opportunities. Remember, you have already observed that this person appears to have had some training and is calm and in control of himself and, therefore, of you. He keeps his distance from you and maintains his shooting stance and sight alignment. You, in turn, are careful to send him only messages of compliance — verbal ones, if necessary. You don't look into his eyes — this can be challenging — but keep a general focus on his whole body. You force yourself to stop looking down the gun barrel, because "gun muzzle hypnosis" can paralyze your thought processes.

The man tells you to move behind the counter next to the store clerks, and to put your purse or wallet on the counter. That's easy enough: He has demanded something that is not worth your life. You comply. He takes the money from the store, plus your wallet, and leaves. You have survived.

Change the scenario a bit: The moment you get inside the store, you realize immediately that, far from being in control of himself, this person is nervous and jumpy. Perhaps he is mentally disturbed or under the effect of drugs, or perhaps something happened just before you came in that angered and frightened him. He is under irresistible time pressure; he doesn't know how long it will be before more witnesses come into the store, or even whether a police patrol will happen along. He is shouting, brandishing the gun in one hand, and he comes up to you and puts the gun right in your face. Because you have no choice at this moment, you are looking at the gun and his hand. You see that his grip is tightening and loosening nervously, and you know he is on the verge of shooting you as he works himself up into a rage. He is out of control.

If you have had some firearms training, you may even be able to judge the condition of the gun. Is the hammer back? If so, whether pistol or revolver, the gun can fire very easily, even by accident. This man, at this moment, is more dangerous by far than the one we described above. Death or serious injury is imminent, and the gun is so close that even an untrained person cannot miss. You need to move, and you need distance, quickly. Although this is the moment when most people freeze, it is, in fact, the time to *resist*. You have nothing whatsoever to lose.

The good news is that this shooter has given you an opportunity, however risky. If you have been lucky enough to have gotten some high-quality self-defense training, you know that if you can get a shooter to come within arm's length, you can at least momentarily get yourself out of the line of fire by acting quickly. You may even have training in disarming a shooter, but if you don't, you still understand that action is always faster than reaction: If you move quickly enough, without telegraphing your motion, you can position your body to the side of and behind the muzzle of the gun before even the most alert shooter can pull the trigger. Raised hands and verbalization are helpful distractions as well.

What happens next depends on your training. You can control the gun (easier than it sounds if you have been taught how) or simply use all the force you have to push the shooter off balance, long enough for you to gain some distance. Again, this is risky, but you have no viable choice: You must resist in order to escape and survive.

Resistance, then, is wise and appropriate when death or serious injury is imminent, when the shooter is not talking or intimidating for compliance. He is already shooting, or is about to shoot at very close range at you or someone you care about.

There is a second circumstance that argues strongly in favor of resistance and against compliance. Crime statistics show overwhelmingly that when a victim is moved from the place of original encounter to a second location — sometimes called the "secondary crime scene" — his or her chances of survival are dramatically reduced. The secondary crime scene is always going to be a place of less safety for the victim and greater safety for the predator to do as he pleases. Victims are well-advised to do everything possible to avoid being taken from the place of initial encounter.

This non-compliance and resistance need not be declared and telegraphed to the criminal, however. In our notional scenario, just suppose that as the criminal leaves the store, he orders you at gunpoint to accompany him to your car, which is parked just outside. You should give every appearance of complying, because as the two of you move to a different environment the situation becomes fluid. There will be two moments when it may be possible to escape during this short journey: when you go through the door, and when the two of you get into the car. Unless the criminal is very calm, experienced and has rehearsed things carefully at least in his mind, these two moments will present him with difficult tactical challenges, challenges that will compromise his ability to keep you always in his gun sights. These are the

140

moments to look for and exploit. A good self-defense course will identify and re-create them in drilled scenarios.

Summing up, you should *comply* when:

- Death or severe physical harm is not imminent.

- The criminal is using his weapon only to intimidate for compliance (although the dynamics can change in an instant, this is the criminal's state of mind at *this* instant).

- What is being demanded is not worth your life (*your* decision).

- There is no immediate opportunity for escape. You need to buy some time and wait for or create an opportunity.

You should *resist and escape* when:

- The criminal does not yet have you under control and a clearly viable escape route exists.

- The attack has begun: The criminal is already shooting.

- The criminal is about to shoot: Death or severe injury is imminent.

- The criminal tries to take you from the place of initial encounter to a less safe place, the "secondary crime scene."

Multiple Attackers

In some kinds of violent confrontations, multiple attackers are more common than otherwise. Except in the case of military-style ambush configurations (which attempt to put their targets in a crossfire), multiple shooters are best treated the same way as a single shooter armed with a shotgun or automatic weapon: The formula MDACC still applies, with the caveat that there is a lot more lead flying around.

Multiple attackers, either empty-handed or with hand weapons other than firearms, present special problems and an enhanced danger of serious injury.

Unless the attacking group has previously coordinated and is experienced in this type of attack, not all of its members will be equally committed to the attack. Someone will take the point, and it is important to identify this person as quickly as possible. Move away from him and toward members of the group who seem less committed. If the attack begins immediately without verbalization, you can assume you are dealing with people who have done this before.

Generally speaking, the greatest number of attackers that can simultaneously reach you while you are on your feet are four: one each, back and front, and one on each side. Any more than that will be getting in each others' way.

When you are down, the number of attackers who now can reach you with their feet more than doubles; thus,

142

the first goal should be to stay on your feet. This is not easy. If you are down, unless you are well-trained in fighting from the ground, it's best to concentrate on protecting yourself against the most serious injuries: to the head, spine and vital organs.

Assuming you are still upright, the second goal is to quickly reduce the number of attackers who can reach you simultaneously. Getting your back to a wall or a large object such as a car will reduce that number to three, and the two at your sides will have their fighting space reduced by half. Try to pick a wall that ends in a door and fight your way toward it, but avoid telegraphing your intentions by turning your head toward it: Someone will be sure to anticipate and block your way.

The better self-defense courses will teach students how to change their own positioning so that attackers "stack up" one behind the other, somewhat like a "pick" in basketball. This technique cannot be sustained for more than a few seconds before attackers figure it out, but it can buy the time needed to get one's back to a wall or to get through a door.

Finally, we will end this analysis as we began it, with caveats. The guidance we give here should never have to be used by people who practice good security awareness. It should be considered as guidance, and perhaps incorporated into one's formal, professional self-defense training scenarios. And, again, resistance against armed attackers must only be considered when there is no viable alternative — when death or severe injury is imminent or highly likely.

Made in the USA
Lexington, KY
28 October 2010